THE CULT OF INCOMPETENCE

By EMILE FAGUET
Of the French Academy

TRANSLATED FROM THE
FRENCH BY
BEATRICE BARSTOW

WITH AN INTRODUCTION BY
THOMAS MACKAY

First Published by E. P. Dutton & Co.
In New York City
1912

Published by Tall Men Books
Summer of 2024
Edited by George Bagby
ISBN: 9798340147981

Tall
Men
Books

Contents

Introduction

Though it may not have been possible in the following pages to reproduce the elegant and incisive style of a master of French prose, not even the inadequacies of a translation can obscure the force of his argument. The only introduction, therefore, that seems possible must take the form of a request to the reader to study M. Faguet's criticism of modern democracy with the daily paper in his hand. He will then see, taking chapter by chapter, how in some aspects the phenomena of English democracy are identical with those described in the text, and how in others our English worship of incompetence, moral and technical, differs considerably from that which prevails in France. It might have been possible, as a part of the scheme of this volume, to note on each page, by way of illustration, instances from contemporary English practice, but an adequate execution of this plan would have overloaded the text, or even required an additional volume. Such a volume, impartially worked out with instances drawn from the programme of all political parties, would be an interesting commentary on current political controversy, and it is to be hoped that M. Faguet's suggestive pages will inspire some competent hand to undertake the task.

If M. Faguet had chosen to refer to England, he might, perhaps, have cited the constitution of this country, as it existed some seventy years ago, as an example of a "demophil aristocracy," raised to power by an "aristocracy-respecting democracy." It is not perhaps wise in political controversy to compromise our liberty of action in respect of the problems of the present time, by too deferential a reference to a golden age which probably, like Lycurgus in the text, p. 73, never existed at all, but it has been often stated, and undoubtedly with a certain amount of truth, that the years between 1832 and 1866 were the only period in English history during which philosophical principles were allowed an important, we cannot say a paramount, authority over English legislation. The characteristic features of the period were a determination to abolish the privileges of the few, which, however, involved no desire to embark on the impossible and inequitable task of creating privileges for the many; a deliberate attempt to extirpate the servile dependence of the old poor law, and a definite abandonment of the plan of distributing economic advantages by eleemosynary state action. This policy was based on the conviction that personal liberty and freedom of private enterprise were the adequate, constructive influences of a progressive civilisation. Too much importance has perhaps been attached to the relatively unimportant question of the freedom of international trade, for this was only part of a general policy of emancipation which had a much more far-reaching scope. Rightly understood the political philosophy of that time, put forward by the competent statesmen who were then trusted by the democracy, proclaimed the principle of liberty and freedom of exchange as the true solvents of the economic problems of the day. This policy remained in force during the ministry of Sir R. Peel and lasted right down to the time of the great budgets of Mr. Gladstone.

If we might venture, therefore, to add another to the definitions of Montesquieu, we might say that the principle animating a liberal constitutional government was liberty, and that this involved a definite plan for enlarging the sphere of liberty as the organising principle of civil society. To what then are we to impute the decadence from this type into which parliamentary government seems now to have fallen? Can we attribute this to neglect or to exaggeration of its animating principle, as suggested in the formula of Montesquieu? It is a question which the reader may find leisure to investigate; we confine ourselves to marking what seem to be some of the stages of decay.

When the forces of destructive radicalism had done their legitimate work, it seemed a time for rest and patience, for administration rather than for fresh legislation and for a pause during which the principles of liberty and free exchange might have been left to organise the equitable distribution of the inevitably increasing wealth of the country. The patience and the conviction which were needed to allow of such a development, rightly or wrongly, were not forthcoming, and politicians and parties have not been wanting to give effect to remedies hastily suggested to and adopted by the people. Political leaders soon came to realise that recent enfranchisements had added a new electorate for whom philosophical principles had no charm. At a later date also, Mr. Gladstone, yielding to a powerful and not over-scrupulous political agitation, suddenly determined to attempt a great constitutional change in the relations between the United Kingdom and Ireland. Whether the transference of the misgovernment of Ireland from London to Dublin would have had results as disastrous or as beneficial as disputants have asserted, may be matter for doubt, but the manner in which the proposal was made certainly had one unfortunate consequence. Mr. Gladstone's action struck a blow at the independence and self-respect, or as M. Faguet terms it, the moral competence of our parliamentary representation from which it has never recovered. Men were called on to abandon, in the course of a few hours, opinions which they had professed for a lifetime and this not as the result of conviction but on the pressure of party discipline. Political feeling ran high. The "Caucus" was called into more active operation.

Political parties began to invent programmes to capture the groundlings. The conservative party, relinquishing its useful function of critic, revived the old policy of eleemosynary doles, and, in an unlucky moment for its future, has encumbered itself with an advocacy of the policy of protection. For strangely enough the democracy, the bestower of power, though developing symptoms of fiscal tyranny and a hatred of liberty in other directions clings tenaciously to freedom of international trade—for the present at least—and it would seem that the electioneering caucus has, in this instance, failed to understand its own business. The doles of the new State-charity were to be given to meet contributions from the beneficiaries, but as the class which for one reason or another is ever in a destitute condition, could not or would not contribute, the only way in which the benevolent purpose of the agitation could be carried out was by bestowing the dole gratuitously. The flood gates, therefore, had to be opened wider, and we have been and still are exposed to a rush of philanthropic legislation which is gradually transferring all the responsibilities of life from the individual to the state. Free trade for the moment remains, and it is supposed to be strongly entrenched in the convictions of the liberal party. Its position, however, is obviously very precarious in view of the demands made by the militant trade unions. These, in their various spheres, claim a monopoly of employment for their members, to the exclusion of those who do not belong to their associations. Logic has something, perhaps not much, to do with political action, and it is almost inconceivable that a party can go on for long holding these two contradictory opinions. Which of them will be abandoned, the future only can tell.

The result of all this is a growing disinclination on the part of the people to limit their responsibilities to their means of discharging them, the creation of a proletariate which in search of maintenance drifts along the line of least resistance, dependence on the government dole. In the end too it must bring about the impoverishment of the state, which is ever being called on to undertake new burdens; for the individual, thus released from obligation to discharge, is still left free to create responsibilities, for which it is now the business of the State to make provision. Under such a system the ability to pay as well as the number of the solvent citizens must continuously decline.

The proper reply to this legislation which we describe as predatory in the sense that we describe the benevolent habits of Robin Hood as predatory, cannot be made by the official opposition which was itself the first to step on the down grade, and which only waits the chances of party warfare to take its turn in providing *panem et circenses* at the charge of the public exchequer. In this way, progress is brought to a standstill by the chronic unwillingness of the rate- and tax-payers to find the money. A truer policy, based on the voluntary action of citizens and capable of indefinite and continuous expansion, finds no support among politicians, for all political parties seem to be held in the grip of the moral and technical incompetence which M. Faguet has so wittily described. The only reply to a government bent on such courses is that which above has been imputed— perhaps without sufficient justification—to the governments of the period 1832-1866; and that reply democracy, as at present advised, will allow no political party to make.

There does not appear, therefore, to be much difference between the situation here and in France, and it is very interesting to notice how in various details there is a very close parallelism between events in this country and those which M. Faguet has described. The position of our Lord Chancellor, who has been bitterly attacked by his own party, in respect of his appointment of magistrates, is very similar to that of M. Barthou, quoted on p. 118. Our judicial system has hitherto been considered free from political partisanship, but very recently and for the first time a minister in his place in parliament, has rightly or wrongly seen fit to call in question the impartiality of our judicial bench, and the suspicion, if, as appears to be the case, it is widely entertained by persons heated in political strife, will probably lead to appointments calculated to ensure reprisals. Astute politicians do not commit themselves to an attack on a venerated institution, till they think they know that that institution is becoming unpopular with the followers who direct their policy. Criminal verdicts also, especially on the eve of an election, are now made liable to revision by ministers scouring the gaols of the country in search of picturesque malefactors whom, with an accompaniment of much philanthropic speech, they proceed to set at liberty. Even the first principles of equity, as ordinarily understood, seem to have lost their authority, when weighed in the balance against the vote of the majority. Very recently the members of an honourable and useful profession represented to a minister that his extension of a scheme of more or less gratuitous relief to a class which hitherto had been able and willing to pay its way, was likely to deprive them of their livelihood. His reply, *inter alia,* contained the argument that the class in question was very numerous and had many votes, and that he doubted whether any one would venture to propose its exclusion except perhaps a member for a university; as a matter of fact some such proposal had been made by one of the university members whose constituents were affected by the proposal. The minister further declared that he did not think that such an amendment could obtain a seconder. The argument seems to impute to our national representatives a cynical disregard of equity, and a blind worship of numbers, which if true, is an instance of moral incompetence quite as remarkable as anything contained in M. Faguet's narrative.

If readers of this volume will take the trouble to annotate their copies with a record of the relevant incidents which meet them every day of their lives, they cannot fail to acknowledge how terribly inevitable is the rise of incompetence to political power. The tragedy is all the more dreadful, when we recognise, as we all must, the high character and ability of the statesmen and politicians who lie under the thrall of this compelling necessity.

This systematic corruption of the best threatens to assume the proportions of a national disaster. It is the system, not the actors in it, which M. Faguet analyses and invites us to deplore.

Chapter 1

THE PRINCIPLES OF FORMS OF GOVERNMENT.

The question has often been asked, what is the animating principle of different forms of government, for each, it is assumed, has its own principle. In other words, what is the general idea which inspires each political system?

Montesquieu, for instance, proved that the *principle* of monarchy is *honour*, the principle of despotism *fear*, the principle of a republic *virtue* or patriotism, and he added with much justice that governments decline and fall as often by carrying their principle to excess, as by neglecting it altogether.

And this, though a paradox, is true. At first sight it may not be obvious how a despotism can fall by inspiring too much fear, or a constitutional monarchy by developing too highly the sentiment of honour, or a republic by having too much virtue. It is nevertheless true.

To make too common a use of fear is to destroy its efficacy. As Edgar Quinet happily puts it: "If we want to make use of fear we must be certain that we can use it always." We cannot have too much honour, but when we can appeal to this sentiment only and when distinctions, decorations, orders, ribbons—in a word *honours*—are multiplied, inasmuch as we cannot increase such things indefinitely, those who have none become as discontented as those who, having some, want more.

Finally we cannot, of course, have too much virtue, and naturally here governments will fall not by exaggerating but by abandoning their guiding principle. Yet is it not sometimes true that by demanding from citizens too great a devotion to their country, we end by exhausting human powers of endurance and sacrifice? This is what happened in the case of Napoleon, who, perhaps unwittingly, required too much from France, for the building up of a 'Greater France.'

But that, some one will object, was not a republic!

From the point of view of the sacrifices required from the citizen, it was a republic, similar to the Roman Republic and to the French Republic of 1792. All the talk was 'for the glory of our country,' 'heroism, heroism, nothing but heroism'! If too much is required of it, civic virtue can be exhausted.

It is, then, very true that governments perish just as much from an excess as from a neglect of their appropriate principle. Montesquieu without doubt borrowed his general idea from Aristotle, who remarks not without humour, "Those, who think that they have discovered the basis of good government, are apt to push the consequences of their new found principle too far. They do not remember that disproportion in such matters is fatal. They forget that a nose which varies slightly from the ideal line of beauty appropriate for noses, tending slightly towards becoming a hook or a snub, may still be of fair shape and not disagreeable to the eye, but if the excess be very great, all symmetry is lost, and the nose at last ceases to be a nose at all." This law of proportion holds good with regard to every form of government.

Starting from these general ideas, I have often wondered what principle democrats have adopted for the form of government which they favour, and it has not required a great effort on my part to arrive at the conclusion that the principle in question is the worship and cultivation, or, briefly 'the cult' of incompetence or inefficiency.

Let us examine any well-managed and successful business firm or factory. Every employee does the work he knows and does best, the skilled workman, the accountant, the manager and the secretary, each in his place. No one would dream of making the accountant change places with a commercial traveller or a mechanic.

Look too at the animal world. The higher we go in the scale of organic existence, the greater the division of labour, the more marked the specialisation of physiological function. One organ thinks, another acts, one digests, another breathes. Now is there such a thing as an animal with only one organ, or rather is there any animal, consisting of only one organ, which breathes and thinks and digests all at the same time? Yes, there is. It is called the amœba, and the amœba is the very lowest thing in the animal world, very inferior even to a vegetable.

In the same way, without doubt, in a well constituted society, each organ has its definite function, that is to say, administration is carried on by those who have learnt how to administer, legislation and the amendment of laws by those who have learnt how to legislate, justice by those who have studied jurisprudence, and the functions of a country postman are not given to a paralytic. Society should model itself on nature, whose plan is specialisation. "For," as Aristotle says, "she is not niggardly, like the Delphian smiths whose knives have to serve for many purposes, she makes each thing for a single purpose, and the best instrument is that which serves one and not many uses." Elsewhere he says, "At Carthage it is thought an honour to hold many offices, but a man only does one thing well. The legislator should see to this, and prevent the same man from being set to make shoes and play the flute." A well-constituted society, we may sum up, is one where every function is not confided to every one, where the crowd itself, the whole body social, is not told: "It is your business to govern, to administer, to make the laws, &c." A society, where things are so arranged, is an amœbic society.

That society, therefore, stands highest in the scale, where the division of labour is greatest, where specialisation is most definite, and where the distribution of functions according to efficiency is most thoroughly carried out.

Now democracies, far from sharing this view, are inclined to take the opposite view. At Athens there was a great tribunal composed of men learned in, and competent to interpret, the law. The people could not tolerate such an institution, so laboured to destroy it and to usurp its functions. The crowd reasoned thus. "We can interpret and carry out laws, because we make them." The conclusion was right, but the minor premise was disputable. The retort can be made: "True, you can interpret and carry out laws because you make them, but perhaps you have no business to be making laws." Be that as it may, the Athenian people not only interpreted and applied its own laws, but it insisted on being paid for so doing. The result was that the poorest citizens sat judging all day long, as all others were unwilling to sacrifice their whole time for a payment of six drachmas. This plebeian tribunal continued for many years. Its most celebrated feat was the judgment which condemned Socrates to death. This was perhaps matter for regret, but the great principle, the sovereignty of incompetence, was vindicated.

Modern democracies seem to have adopted the same principle, in form they are essentially amœbic. A democracy, well-known to us all, has been evolved in the following manner.

It began with this idea; king and people, democratic royalty, royal democracy. The people makes, the king carries out, the law; the people legislates, the king governs, retaining, however, a certain control over the law, for he can suspend the carrying out of a new law when he considers that it tends to obstruct the function of government. Here then was a sort of specialisation of functions. The same person, or collective body of persons, did not both legislate and govern.

This did not last long. The king was suppressed. Democracy remained, but a certain amount of respect for efficiency remained too. The people, the masses, did not, every single man of them, claim the right to govern and to legislate directly.

It did not even claim the right to nominate the legislature directly. It adopted indirect election, *à deux degrés*, that is, it nominated electors who in turn nominated the legislature. It thus left two aristocracies above itself, the first electors and the elected legislature. This was still far removed from democracy on the Athenian model which did everything itself.

This does not mean that much attention was paid to efficiency. The electors were not chosen because they were particularly fitted to elect a legislature, nor was the legislature itself elected with any reference to its legislative capacity. Still there was a certain pretence of a desire for efficiency, a double pseudo-efficiency. The crowd, or rather the constitution, assumed that legislators elected by the delegates of the crowd were more competent to make laws than the crowd itself.

This somewhat curious form of efficiency I have called *compétence par collation*, efficiency or competence conferred by this form of selection. There is absolutely nothing to show that so-and-so has the slightest legislative or juridical faculty, so I confer on him a certificate of efficiency by the confidence I repose in him when nominating him for the office, or rather I show my confidence in the electors and they confer a certificate of efficiency on those whom they nominate for the legislature.

This, of course, is devoid of all common sense, but appearances, and even something more, are in its favour.

It is not common sense for it involves something being made out of nothing, inefficiency producing efficiency and zero extracting 'one' out of itself. This form of selection, though it does not appeal to me under any circumstances, is legitimate enough when it is exercised by a competent body. A university can confer a degree upon a distinguished man because it can judge whether his degreeless condition is due to accident or not. It would, however, be highly ridiculous and paradoxical if the general public were to confer mathematical degrees. A degree of efficiency conferred by an inefficient body is contrary to common sense.

There is, however, some plausibility and indeed a little more than plausibility in favour of this plan. Degrees in literature and in dramatic art are conferred, given by 'collation,' by incompetent people, that is by the public. We can say to the public: "You know nothing of literary and dramatic art." It will retort: "True, I know nothing, but certain things move me and I confer the degree on those who evoke my emotions." In this it is not altogether wrong. In the same way the degree of doctor of political science is conferred by the people on those who stir its emotions and who express most forcibly its own passions. These doctors of political science are the empassioned representatives of its own passions.

—In other words, the worst legislators!—

Yes, very nearly so, but not quite. It is very useful that we should have an exponent of popular passion at the crest of the social wave, to tell us not indeed what the crowd is thinking, for the crowd never thinks, but what the crowd is feeling, in order that we may not cross it too violently or obey it too obsequiously. An engineer would call it the science of the strength of materials.

A medium assures me that he had a conversation with Louis XIV, who said to him: "Universal suffrage is an excellent thing in a monarchy. It is a source of information. When it recommends a certain course of action it shows us that this is a thing which we must not do. If I could have consulted it over the Revocation of the Edict of Nantes, it would have given me a clear mandate for that Revocation and I should have known what to do, and that Edict would not have been revoked. I acted as I did, because I was advised by ministers whom I considered experienced statesmen. Had I been aware of the state of public opinion I should have known that France was tired of wars and new palaces and extravagance. But this was not an expression of passion and prejudice, but a cry of suffering. As far as passion and prejudice are concerned we must go right in the teeth of public opinion, and universal suffrage will tell you what that is. On the other hand we must pay heed, serious heed to every cry of pain, and here too universal suffrage will come to our aid. Universal suffrage is necessary to a monarchy as a source of information."

This, I am told, is Louis XIV's present opinion on the subject.

As far as legislation therefore is concerned, the attempt to secure competence by 'collation' is an absurdity. Yet it is an inverted sort of competence useful for indicating the state of a nation's temper. From this it follows that this system is as mischievous in a republic as it would be wholesome in a monarchy. It is not therefore altogether bad.

The democracy which we have in view, after having been governed by the representatives of its representatives for ten years, submitted for the next fifteen years to the rule of one representative and took no particular advantage therefrom.

Then for thirty years it adopted a scheme which aimed at a certain measure of efficiency. It assumed that the electors of the legislature ought not to be nominated, but marked out by their social position, that is their fortune. Those who possessed so many drachmas were to be electors.

What sort of a basis for efficiency is this? It is a basis but certainly a somewhat narrow one.

It is a basis, first, because a man who owns a certain fortune has a greater interest than others in a sound management of public business, and self-interest opens and quickens the eye; and again a man who has money and does not lose it cannot be altogether a fool.

On the other hand it is a narrow basis, because the possession of money is of itself no guarantee of political ability, and the system leads to the very questionable proposition that every rich man is a competent social reformer. It is, however, a sort of competence, but a competence very precariously established and on a very narrow basis.

This system disappeared and our democracy, after a short interregnum, repeated its previous experiment and submitted for eighteen years to the rule of one delegate with no great cause to congratulate itself on the result.

It then adopted democracy in a form almost pure and simple. I say almost, for the democratic system pure and simple involves the direct government of the people without any intervening representatives, by means of a continuous plebiscite. Our democracy then set up and still maintains a democratic system almost pure and simple, that is to say, it established government of the nation by delegates whom it itself elected and by these delegates strictly and exclusively. This time we have reached an apotheosis of incompetence that is well nigh absolute.

This, our present system, purports to be the rule of efficiency chosen by the arbitrary form of selection which has been described. Just as the bishop in the story, addressing a haunch of venison, exclaimed: "I baptise thee carp," so the people says to its representatives: "I baptise you masters of law, I baptise you statesmen, I baptise you social reformers." We shall see later on that this baptism goes very much further than this.

If the people were capable of judging of the legal and psychological knowledge possessed by those who present themselves for election, this form of selection need not be prohibitive of efficiency and might even be satisfactory; but in the first place, the electors are not capable of judging, and secondly, even if they were, nothing would be gained.

Nothing would be gained, because the people never places itself at this point of view. Emphatically never! It looks at the qualifications of the candidate not from a scientific but from a moral point of view.

—Well that surely is something, and, in a way, a guarantee of efficiency. The legislators are not capable of making laws, it is true; but at least they are honest men. This guarantee of moral efficiency, some critic will say, gives me much satisfaction.

Please be careful, I reply, we should never think of giving the management of a railway station to the most honest man, but to an honest man who, besides, understood thoroughly railway administration. So we must put into our laws not only honest intentions, but just principles of law, politics, and society.

Secondly, if the candidates are considered from the point of view of their moral worth it is in a peculiar fashion. High morality is imputed to those who share the dominant passions of the people and who express themselves thereon more violently than others. Ah! these are our honest men, it cries, and I do not say that the men of its choice are dishonest, I only say that by this criterion they are not infallibly marked out even as honest.

—Still, some one replies, they are probably disinterested, for they follow popular prejudices, and not their own particular, individual wishes.

Yes, that is just what the masses believe, while they forget that there is nothing easier than to simulate popular passion in order to win popular confidence and become a political personage. If disinterestedness is really so essential to the people, only those should be elected who oppose the popular will and who show thereby that they do not want to be elected. Or better still only those who do not stand for election should be elected, since not to stand is the undeniable sign of disinterestedness. But this is never done. That which should always be done is never done.

—But, some one will say, your public bodies which recruit their numbers by co-optation, Academies and learned societies, do not elect their members in this way.—

Quite so, and they are right. Such bodies do not want their members to be disinterested but scientific. They have no reason to prefer an unwilling member to one who is eager to be elected. Their point of view is entirely different. The people, which pretends to set store by high moral character, should exclude from power those who are ambitious of power, or at least those who covet it with a keenness that suggests other than disinterested motives.

These considerations show us what the crowd understands by the moral worth of a man. The moral worth of a man consists, as far as the crowd is concerned, in his entertaining or pretending to entertain the same sentiments as itself, and it is just for this reason that the representatives of the multitude are excellent as documents for information, but detestable, or at least, useless, and therefore detestable, as legislators.

Montesquieu, who is seldom wrong, errs in my opinion when he says, "The people is well-fitted to choose its own magistrates." He, it is true, did not live under a democracy. For consider, how could the people be fitted to choose its own magistrates and legislators, when Montesquieu himself, this time with ample justification, lays down as one of his principles that morals should correct climate, and that law should correct morals, and the people, as we know, only thinks of choosing as its delegates men who share, in every particular, its own manner of thinking? Climate can be partially resisted by the people; but if the law should correct morals, legislators should be chosen who have taken up an attitude of reaction against current morality. It would be very curious if such a choice were ever made, and not only is it never made but the contrary invariably happens.

To sum it all up, it is intellectual incompetence, nay moral incompetence which is sought instinctively in the people's choice.

If possible, it is more than this. The people favours incompetence, not only because it is no judge of intellectual competence and because it looks on moral competence from a wrong point of view, but because it desires before everything, as indeed is very natural, that its representatives should resemble itself. This it does for two reasons.

First, as a matter of sentiment, the people desires, as we have seen, that its representatives should share its feelings and prejudices. These representatives can share its prejudices and yet not absolutely resemble it in morals, habits, manners and appearance; but naturally the people never feels so certain that a man shares its prejudices and is not merely pretending to do so, as when the man resembles it feature by feature. It is a sign and a guarantee. The people is instinctively impelled therefore to elect men of the same habits, manners and even education as itself, or shall we say of an education slightly superior, the education of a man who can talk, but only superior in a very slight degree.

In addition to this sentimental reason, there is another, which is extremely important, for it goes to the very root of the democratic idea. What is the people's one desire, when once it has been stung by the democratic tarantula? It is that all men should be equal, and in consequence that all inequalities natural as well as artificial should disappear. It will not have artificial inequalities, nobility of birth, royal favours, inherited wealth, and so it is ready to abolish nobility, royalty, and inheritance. Nor does it like natural inequalities, that is to say a man more intelligent, more active, more courageous, more skilful than his neighbours. It cannot destroy these inequalities, for they are natural, but it can neutralise them, strike them with impotence by excluding them from the employments under its control. Democracy is thus led quite naturally, irresistibly one may say, to exclude the competent precisely because they are competent, or if the phrase pleases better and as the popular advocate would put it, not because they are competent but because they are unequal, or, as he would probably go on to say, if he wished to excuse such action, not because they are unequal, but because being unequal they are suspected of being opponents of equality. So it all comes to the same thing. This it is that made Aristotle say that where merit is despised, there is democracy. He does not say so in so many words, but he wrote: "Where merit is not esteemed before everything else, it is not possible to have a firmly established aristocracy," and that amounts to saying that where merit is not esteemed, we enter at once on a democratic regime and never escape from it.

The chance, then, of efficiency coming to the front in this state of affairs is indeed deplorable.

First and last, democracy—and it is natural enough—*wishes to do everything itself,* it is the enemy of all specialisation of functions, particularly it wishes to govern, without delegates or intermediaries. Its ideal is direct government as it existed at Athens, its ideal is "democracy," in the terminology of Rousseau, who applied the word to direct government and to direct government only.

Forced by historical events and perhaps by necessity to govern by delegates, how could democracy still contrive to govern directly or nearly so, although continuing to govern through delegates?

Its first alternative is, perhaps, to impose on its delegates an imperative mandate. Delegates under this condition become mere agents of the people. They attend the legislative assembly to register the will of the people just as they receive it, and the people in reality governs directly. This is what is meant by the imperative mandate.

Democracy has often considered it, but never with persistence. Herein it shows good sense. It has a shrewd suspicion that the imperative mandate is never more than a snare and a delusion. Representatives of the people meet and discuss, the interests of party become defined. Henceforward they are the prey of the goddess Opportunity, the Greek Καιρός Καιρός. Then it happens one day that to vote according to their mandate would be very unfavourable to the interest of their party. They are therefore obliged to be faithless to their party by reason of their fidelity to their mandate, or disobedient to their mandate by reason of their obedience to their party; and in any case to have betrayed their mandate with this very praiseworthy and excellent intention is a thing for which they can take credit or at least obtain excuse with the electors—and on such a matter it will be very difficult to refute them.

The imperative mandate is therefore a very clumsy instrument for work of a very delicate character. The democracy, instinctively, knows this very well, and sets no great store by the imperative mandate.

What other alternative is there for it? Something very much finer, the substance instead of the shadow. It can elect men who resemble it closely, who follow its sentiments closely, who are in fact so nearly identical with itself that they may be trusted to do surely, instinctively, almost mechanically that which it would itself do, if it were itself an immense legislative assembly. They would vote, without doubt, according to circumstances, but also as their electors would vote if they were governing directly. In this way democracy preserves its legislative power. It makes the law, and this is the only way it can make it.

Democracy, therefore, has the greatest inducement to elect representatives who are representative, who, in the first place, resemble it as closely as possible, who, in the second place, have no individuality of their own, who finally, having no fortune of their own, have no sort of independence.

We deplore that democracy surrenders itself to politicians, but from its own point of view, a point of view which it cannot avoid taking up, it is absolutely right. What is a politician? He is a man who, in respect of his personal opinions, is a nullity, in respect of education, a mediocrity, he shares the general sentiments and passions of the crowd, his sole occupation is politics, and if that career were closed to him, he would die of starvation.

He is precisely the thing of which the democracy has need.

He will never be led away by his education to develop ideas of his own; and having no ideas of his own, he will not allow them to enter into conflict with his prejudices. His prejudices will be, at first by a feeble sort of conviction, afterwards by reason of his own interest, identical with those of the crowd; and lastly, his poverty and the impossibility of his getting a living outside of politics make it certain that he will never break out of the narrow circle where his political employers have confined him; his imperative mandate is the material necessity which obliges him to obey; his imperative mandate is his inability to quarrel with his bread and butter.

Democracy obviously has need of politicians, has need of nothing else but politicians, and has need indeed that there shall be in politics nothing else but politicians.

Its enemy, or rather the man whom democracy dreads because he means to govern and does not intend to allow the mob to govern through him, is the man who succeeds in getting elected for some constituency or other, either by the influence of his wealth or by the prestige of his talent and notoriety. Such a man is not dependent on democracy. If a legislative assembly were entirely or by a majority composed of rich men, men of superior intelligence, men who had an interest in attending to the trades or professions in which they had succeeded rather than in playing at politics, they would vote according to their own ideas, and then—what would happen? Why then democracy would be simply suppressed. It would no longer legislate and govern; there would be, to speak exactly, an aristocracy, not very permanently established perhaps, but still an aristocracy which would eliminate the influence of the people from public affairs.

Clearly it is almost impossible for the democracy, if it means to survive, to encourage efficiency, nay it is almost impossible for it to refrain from attempting to destroy efficiency.

Thus, we may sum up, only those are elected as the representatives of the people, who are its exact counterparts and constant dependents.

CHAPTER II.
CONFUSION OF FUNCTIONS.

And what is the result of all this? The result, which is very logical, very just from the democratic point of view, and precisely that which the democracy desires and cannot do otherwise than desire, is that the national representatives do exactly what the people would wish them to do, and what the people would do itself if it undertook to govern directly itself. *The representative government wishes to do everything itself*, just as the people would like to do, if it were itself exercising the functions of government directly, just as it did in olden times on the Pnyx at Athens.

Montesquieu realised this fully, though naturally he had no experience of how the theory worked under a representative and parliamentary system. The principle of it all is at bottom the same, and only the change of a single phrase is needed to make the following quotation strictly applicable. "The principle of democracy," he says, "is perverted not only when it loses the spirit of equality, but still more *when it carries the spirit of equality to an extreme, and when every one wishes to be the equal of those whom he chooses to govern him.* For then the people, not being able to tolerate the authority which it has created, *wishes to do everything itself*, to deliberate for the Senate, to act for the magistrates, and to usurp the functions of the judges. The people wishes to exclude the magistrates from their functions, and the magistrates naturally are no longer respected. The deliberations of the Senate are allowed to have no weight, and senators naturally fall into contempt."

Let us translate the foregoing passage into the language of to-day. Under democratic parliamentary government the representatives of the people are determined to do everything themselves. They must be equal to those whom they choose for their rulers. They cannot tolerate the authority which they have entrusted to the Government. They must themselves govern in the place of the Government, administer in the place of the executive staff, substitute their own authority for that of all the bench of judges, perform the duties of magistrates, and, in a word, throw off all regard and respect for persons and things.

This is the true inwardness of the popular spirit, the will of the people which wishes to do everything itself, or what is the same thing, through its representatives, its faithful and servile creatures.

From this point onwards efficiency is hunted and exterminated in every direction; just as it was excluded in the election of representatives, so the representatives laboriously and continuously exclude it from every sort of office and employment under the public service.

The Government, to begin our analysis of functional confusion at the top, ought to be watched and advised by the national representatives, but it ought to be independent of the national representatives, at least it ought not to be inextricably mixed up with them, in other words the national representatives ought not to govern. Under democracy this is precisely what they want to do. They elect the Government, a privilege which need not be denied them; but, "not being able to tolerate the authority which they have created," as soon as they have set it up, they put pressure on it and insist on governing continuously in its place. The assembly of national representatives is not a body which makes laws, but a body which, by a never ending string of questions and interruptions, *dictates* from day to day to the Government what it ought to do, that is to say, it is a body which governs.

The country is governed, literally, by the Chamber of Deputies. *This is absolutely necessary* if, as the true spirit of the system requires, the people is to be governed by no one but itself, if there is to be no will at work other than the will of the people, emanating from itself and bringing back a sort of harvest of executive acts. Again, I repeat, this is absolutely necessary, in order that there shall be nothing, not even originating with the people, which, for a single moment and within the most narrowly defined limits, shall exercise the functions of sovereignty over the sovereign people.

This is all very well, but government is an art and we assume that there is a science of government, and here we have the people governed by persons who have neither science nor art, and who are chosen precisely because they have not these qualifications and on the guarantee that they have none of them!

Again, in a democracy of this kind, if there exist, as a result of tradition or of some necessity arising out of foreign relations, an authority, independent for a certain term of years of the legislative assembly, which has no accounts to render to it and which cannot be questioned or constitutionally overthrown, that authority is so strange, and, if the phrase may pass, so monstrous an anomaly, that it dares not exercise its power, and dreads the scandal which it would raise by acting on its rights, and seems as it were paralysed with terror at the very thought of its own existence.

And its attitude is right; for if it exercised its powers, or even lent itself to any appearance of so doing, there at once would be an act of will which was not an act of the popular will, a theory altogether contrary to the spirit of this system. For in this system the chief of the state can only be the nominal chief of the state. A will of his own would be an abuse of power, an idea of his own would be an encroachment, and a word of his own would be an act of high treason.

It follows that, if the constitution has formally conferred these powers, the constitution on these points is a dead letter, because it contravenes an unwritten constitution of higher authority, viz., the inner inspiration of the political institution.

One of these honorary chiefs of the state has said: "During all my term as president, I was constitutionally silent." This is not correct, for the constitution gave him leave to speak and even to act. At bottom it was true, for the constitution, in allowing him to act and speak, was acting unconstitutionally. In speaking he would have been constitutional, in holding his tongue he was *institutional*. He had been in fact *institutionally* silent. He disobeyed the letter of the constitution, but he had admirably extracted its meaning from it, and understood and respected its spirit.

Under democracy, then, the national representatives govern as directly and as really as possible, dictating a policy to the executive and neutralising the supreme chief of the executive to whom it is not able to dictate.

The national representatives are not content with governing, they wish to administer.

Now consider how it would be if the permanent officials of finance, justice and police, etc., depended solely on their parliamentary chiefs, who are ministers only because they are the creatures of the popular assembly, liable to instant and frequent dismissal; surely then, these officials, more permanent than their chiefs, would form an aristocracy, and would administer the state independently of the popular will and according to their own ideas.

This, of course, must not be allowed to happen. There must not be any will but the people's will, no other power, however limited, but its own.

This causes a dilemma which is sufficiently remarkable. Here we seem to have contrary results from the same cause. Since the popular assembly governs ministers, and frequently dismisses them, they are not able to govern their subordinates as did Colbert and Louvois, and these subordinates accordingly are very independent; so it comes about that the greater the authority which the popular assembly wields over ministers, the more it is likely to lose in its control over the subordinates of ministers, and in destroying one rival power it creates another.

The dilemma, however, is avoided easily enough. No public official is appointed without receiving its *visa*, and it contrives even to elect the administrative officials. In the first place, the national representatives, in their corporate capacity, and in the central offices of government, watch most attentively the appointment of the permanent staff, and further each single member of the representative government in his province, in his department, in his *arrondissement* picks and chooses the candidates and really appoints the permanent staff. This is, of course, necessary, if the national will is to be paramount here as well as elsewhere, and if the people is to secure servants of its own type, if it is "to choose its own magistrates," as Montesquieu said.

The people, then, chooses its servants through the intervention of its representatives; and consider, to return to our point, how absolutely necessary it is for it to secure representatives who are intellectually the exact image and imitation of itself. Everything dovetails neatly together.

Here then we have the people interfering influentially in the appointment of the civil service. It continues "to do everything itself." Complaints are raised on all sides of this confusion of politics with the business of administration, and indeed we hear continually that politics pervade everything. But what is the reason of this? It is the principle of the national sovereignty asserting itself. Politics, political power, means the will of the majority of the nation, and is it not fitting that the will of the majority should make itself felt—indeed need we be surprised that it insists on making itself felt—in the details of public business, as administered by the permanent staff, as well as elsewhere? The ideal of democracy is that the people should elect its own rulers, or, if this is not its ideal, it is its idea, and this is what it does under a parliamentary democracy through the intervention of its representatives.

This is all very well, but efficiency has been dealt another blow. For how is a candidate to recommend himself for an office to which appointment is made by the people and its representatives? By his merit? His chiefs and his fellow civil servants might be good judges of that; but the people or its representatives are much less capable of judging.

"The people is admirably fitted to choose those to whom it has to entrust some part of its authority"; so Montesquieu; we must now examine this saying a little more closely. What reasons does the philosopher give? "The people can only be guided by things of which it cannot be ignorant, and which fall, so to speak, within its own observation. It knows very well that a man has experience in war, and that he has had such and such successes; it is therefore quite capable of electing a general. It knows that a judge is industrious, that many of those who are litigants in his court go away satisfied, and that he has never been convicted of bribery, and this is enough to warrant it in appointing to any judicial office. It has been impressed by the magnificence or riches of some citizen, and this fits it for appointing an ædile. All these things are matters of fact about which the man in the street has better knowledge than the king in his palace."

This passage, I confess, does not appear to be convincing. Why should not a king in his palace know of the riches of a financier, the reputation of a judge or the success of a colonel just as well as the man in the street? There is no difficulty in getting information about such things. The people knows that such an one was always a good judge and such another always an excellent officer. Therefore it is qualified to appoint a general or a high-court judge or other officer of the law. So be it, but for the selection of a young judge or a young and untried officer what special source of information has the people? I cannot find that it has any. In this very argument, Montesquieu limits the competence of the people to the election of the great chiefs, and of the most exalted magistrates, and indeed further confines the popular prerogative in this matter to assigning an office and career to one who has already given proof of his capacity. But for putting the competent man for the first time in the place where he is wanted, how has the people any special instinct or information? Montesquieu shows that the people can recognise ability when it has been proved, but he says nothing to show that it recognises readily nascent, unproved talent. The argument of Montesquieu is not here conclusive.

He has been led astray, it seems to me, by his desire to present his argument antithetically (using the term in its logical sense). What he really wished to prove was not so much the truth of the proposition that he was then advancing, but the falsity of quite another proposition. The question for him, the question which he had in his mind, was as follows: Is the people capable of governing the state, of taking measures beforehand, and of understanding and solving the difficulties of home and foreign affairs? By no means. Then is it fit to elect its own magistrates?

Well, it might do that. Thus he had been led away by this antithesis so far as to say: Able to govern?—Certainly not! Able to elect its own magistrates? Admirably! The explanation of the whole paragraph which I have just quoted lies in the conclusion, which runs as follows: "All these things are matters of fact about which the man in the street has better knowledge than the king in his palace. *But* can the people pursue a policy and know how to avail itself of the places, occasions, and times when action will be profitable? No! certainly not."

The truth is that the people is a little better fitted to choose a magistrate than to undertake a policy for the gradual humbling of the House of Austria. But not very much so, as it is only a little more difficult to humble the House of Austria, than it is to discover the man who is able to do it.

The masses are particularly incapable of making initial appointments and of giving promotion in the early stages of a career to those who deserve it. Yet in a democracy this is what they are constantly doing.

Again, by what means has the candidate for civil service employment, who is favoured by the people and its representatives, earned their approval? By his merit, of which the people and its representatives are very bad judges? No! By what then? By his conformity to the general views of the people; that is, by the subserviency of his political opinions. The political opinions of a candidate for civil service employment are the only things which mark him out to the popular choice because they are the only subjects on which the people is a good judge.

Yes, but the subserviency of his political opinions may be combined with real merit. True, but this is a mere matter of chance. The people is not, perhaps, in this particular matter consciously hostile to efficiency, rather it is indifferent, or ignores the qualification altogether. Indeed, there is no great compliment paid to efficiency in such transactions.

Here is what inevitably happens. The candidate for a permanent appointment who is not conscious of possessing any particular merit is not slow to realise that it is by his political opinions that he will succeed, and he naturally professes those which are wanted. The candidate who is conscious of merit, very often knowing very well what less meritorious competitors are about, and not wishing to be beaten, also professes the same useful opinions. There we have that "infection of evil," which M. Renouvier has explained so admirably in his *Science de la Morale*.

First, then, we see how most of the candidates chosen by the mandatories of the people are incapable; others who are chosen in spite of their capacity are men of indifferent character; and character, we must admit, in all or nearly all public careers is a necessary part of efficiency.

There remains a small number of meritorious persons who have never identified themselves with current political opinions, and who have slipped into public employment, thanks to some brief moment of inattention on the part of the politicians. These intruders sometimes get on by the mere force of circumstances, but they never reach the highest posts which are always reserved, as indeed is proper and fitting, for those in whom the people has put its trust.

This is how the people administers as well as governs through the intervention of the representative system, dictating to ministers the policy and the details of government.

—I realise, some one here will object, that administrators are nominated by the people, but I do not see how the affairs of the country are actually administered by the people.—

Well, I will tell you. In the first place, by nominating officials it is already far on the road to controlling them, for it infuses into the body of the permanent civil service the spirit of the people to the exclusion of every other source of inspiration, and effectually prevents the civil service from becoming an aristocracy as otherwise it has always a tendency to do. Next, the people does not confine itself to electing its administrators, it watches and spies on them, keeps them in leading strings, and just as the popular representatives dictate to ministers the details of government, so also they dictate to administrators the details of administration.

A *préfet*, a *procureur-général*, an engineer-in-chief under democratic rule is a much harassed man. He has to play his own hand against his ministerial chief and the deputies of his district. He ought to obey the minister, but he has also to obey the deputies of the district which he administers. In this connection curious points arise and situations not a little complicated. The *préfet* owes obedience to the deputies and to the minister, and the minister obeys the deputies, and it might therefore have been supposed that there was only one will, the will which the *préfet* obeyed. But what the minister has to obey is the general will of the popular representatives, and it is this will that he transmits for the allegiance of the *préfet*; but then the *préfet* finds himself colliding against the individual wills of the deputies of his district. The result is what we may call conflicts of obedience which have extraordinary interest for the psychologist, but which are less agreeable for the *préfet*, the engineer-in-chief, or the *procureur-général*.

We note then, in the first place, how everything concurs to make the representative of the popular will as incompetent as he is omnipotent. Incompetent he undoubtedly is, as we have already seen, to start with, and *if he were not so already*, he would certainly become so by reason of the trade or rather of the miscellaneous assortment of trades which are thrust upon him. The surest way of making a man incompetent is to make him Jack-of-all-trades, for then he will be master of none. In the next place, the representative of the popular will and spirit, besides his trade of legislator, has to cross-examine ministers and to dictate to them the details of their duty, that is to say, he has to busy himself in all home and foreign politics. He has also to administer, by choosing and watching administrators and by controlling and inspiring their actions. Without saying anything of the small individual services which it is his interest to render to his constituents and which his constituents are by no means backward in demanding, he looks on himself as responsible for the conduct of things in general. He becomes a sort of universal foreman, not a man, but a man-orchestra, a busybody, so busy that he can apply himself to nothing. He cannot study, or think, or investigate, or, to speak accurately, acquire any sense at all.

If he be efficient in some particular subject, when he enters on his public career, he becomes hopelessly inefficient in all subjects after a few years of public life, and then, void of all individuality, he remains nothing but a public man, that is, a man representing the popular will and never thinking, or able to think, of anything but how to make that will prevail.

And, to press the point again, this is all that is wanted of him; for can you conceive a representative of the popular will, who had somehow preserved a measure of competence in financial or judicial administration, who would prefer, before other candidates, not a political partisan but a man of merit, knowledge and aptitude, and who would even approve in an administrator not acts of political partiality but acts that are just and in conformity with the interests of the state? Why! Such a man would be a detestable servant in the eyes of democracy.

Yes, and I have known such a man. He was not wanting in intelligence or wit and he was honest. A lawyer, he was naturally interested in politics. For local reasons he had failed to be elected as deputy or as senator. Tired of fighting, he obtained a judicial appointment by the influence of his political friends. He became president of court. A case was brought before him where the accused, a person not perhaps of altogether blameless life, was clearly not guilty of any indictable offence. The accused, however, a former *préfet*, appointed by a government now become very unpopular, and known as a reactionary and an aristocrat, was pursued by the animosity of the whole democratic population of the town and province. The president, in the face of openly expressed hostility in court, acquitted him. In the evening the president remarked, not without a touch of humour: "There, that serves them right for not making me a senator!" In other words: "If they had accepted me as a politician, they would have made me a fool, or at least paralysed my efficiency. But they would not have it; so here I am, a man who knows the law and applies it. So much the worse for them!"

"By making a man a slave Zeus took from him half his soul." So Homer. By making a man a politician, Demos takes from him his whole soul, and in omitting to make him a politician, it is foolish enough to leave him his soul.

This is why Demos hates a permanent civil service. An irremovable magistrate or functionary is a man whom the constitution sets free from the grip of the populace. An irremovable official is a man enfranchised, a free man. Demos does not love free men.

This will explain why in every nation where it is paramount, democracy suspends from time to time the irremovable independent official element wherever it is found. The object is nominally to clarify and filter the *personnel* of the official world; but really it is intended to teach the officials whom it spares, that their permanence is only very relative and that, like every one else, they have to reckon with the sovereignty of the people which will turn and rend them if they venture to be too independent.

According to the constitution of 1873 there were irremovable senators in France. In the interest of good government, this was perhaps a sound arrangement. The irremovable senators, in the scheme of the constitution, were intended to be, and in fact were, political and administrative veterans from whose knowledge, efficiency and experience their colleagues were to profit. The plan, from this point of view, might have worked well if the irremovable senators had not been elected by their colleagues but had become so by right; for example every former President of the Republic, every former president of the *Cour de Cassation*, every former president of the Court of Appeal, every admiral, every archbishop might *ex officio* have been raised to the rank of senator for life. From the democratic point of view, however, it was regarded as a positive outrage that there should exist a representative of the people who had not to render account to the people, a representative of the people who had nothing to fear from the accidents of re-election, no risk of failing to secure re-election, in other words that a man should be elected for his supposed efficiency, in no sense representing the people but himself alone.

Permanent senators were abolished. Obviously they constituted a political aristocracy, founded on the pretence of services rendered, and the Senate which elected them also fell under the taint of aristocratic leanings since at that time it recruited its members by co-optation. This of course could not be tolerated.

CHAPTER III.
THE REFUGES OF
EFFICIENCY.

Will efficiency then, you may well ask, when driven out of all public employment, find refuge somewhere? Certainly it will. In private employments and in employments paid by public companies. Barristers, solicitors, doctors, business men, manufacturers and authors are not paid by the state, nor are engineers, mechanics, railway employees; and so far from their efficiency being a bar to their employment, it is their most valuable asset. When a man consults his lawyer or his medical adviser he obviously has no interest in their politics, and when a railway company chooses an engineer, it enquires into his qualifications and ability and is quite indifferent as to whether his political views coincide with the general mentality of the people.

It is for this reason, or at least partly for this reason, that democracy tries to nationalise all employment, as a step in the direction of the nationalisation of everything. For instance it can partly nationalise the medical profession by establishing appointments for doctors, at relief offices, schools, and *lycées*. It can also partly nationalise the legal profession by appointing state-paid professors of law.

Already the State has considerable control over this class of person, for most of them have relations in government employment, whom they do not wish to bring into bad odour by seeming hostile to the opinions of the majority. The State, however, wants to hold them in still tighter control by seizing every opportunity of nationalising and socialising them more completely.

The State wants also to destroy all large associations, and to absorb their activities. The state purchase of a railway, for instance, is, in the first place, a means of exploiting the company; for there is always a hope that the State will be able to filch something out of the transaction; but its chief recommendation lies in the fact that it suppresses a whole army of the company's officials and employees, who were under no obligation to please the Government, and who had no other interest but to do their work properly. The State will thus transform this free population into government employees, whose primary duty is to be docile and subservient.

Under the extreme form and under the complete form of this regime, that is to say under socialism, everyone will be a government official.

Consequently, say the Socialist theorists, all the alleged drawbacks above mentioned will disappear. The State, the democracy, the dominant party, whatever you choose to call it, will no longer be obliged to select its servants, as you say it does, by reason of their subservience and their incompetence, because every citizen will be an official. Thus too will disappear that dual social system, under which half the population lives on the State, while the other half is independent, and prides itself on its superiority in character, in intelligence and in efficiency. Socialism solves the problem.

I do not agree. Under socialism, the electoral system, and, therefore, the party system will still exist. The citizens will choose the legislators, the legislators will choose the Government, and the Government will choose the directors of labour and the distributors of the means of subsistence. Parties, that is, combinations of interests, will still exist, and each party will want to capture the legislature in order to secure the election, from its own number, of the directors of labour and the distributors of the means of subsistence. These directors and distributors will be the new aristocrats of socialism, and they will be expected to arrange "soft jobs" and ampler rations for the members of their own group or party.

Except that wealth and the last vestiges of liberty have been suppressed, nothing has been changed, and all the objections above mentioned still hold. There is no solution here.

If it were a solution, then the socialist government could not long remain elective. It would have to reign by divine right, like the Jesuits in Paraguay. It would have to be a despotism, not only in its policy but in its origin, in fact a monarchy. No intelligent king has any inducement to choose incompetent men as his officials. His interest would lead him to do exactly the opposite. You will say that an intelligent king is a very rare, even an abnormal thing. I readily agree. Except in a very few instances, which history records with amazement, a king has exactly the same reasons as the people for selecting as his favourites men who will not eclipse nor contradict him, and who consequently seldom turn out to be the best of citizens either in respect of intelligence or character. Elective socialism and despotic socialism have the same faults as democracy as we understand the term.

Besides, in truth, the drift of democracy towards socialism is nothing but a reversion to despotism. If socialism were established, it would begin by being elective, and as every elective system lives and breathes and has its being in the party system, the dominant party would elect the legislature, consequently it would constitute the Government and would extort from that Government, simply because it has the power to extort it, every conceivable form of privilege. Exploitation of the country by the majority would result, as in every country where elective government prevails.

A socialist government therefore is primarily an oligarchy of directors of labour and distributors of subsistence. It is a very close oligarchy, for those beneath it are quite defenceless, levelled down to an equality of poverty and misery. It is a form of government very difficult to replace, for it holds in its hands the threads of such an intricate organisation that it must be protected against crude attempts to change it, and so it tends to be a permanent oligarchy. It would therefore concentrate very quickly round a leader, or at any rate, relegate to the second rank the national representatives and the electorate.

Such a course of events would be very similar to what occurred under the First Empire in France, when the military caste eclipsed and domineered over everything. It became continuously necessary to the State, and though that necessity passed away, it was soon recalled. The caste then closed its ranks round the leader who gave it unity, and the strength of unity.

So under socialism, more slowly and perhaps after the lapse of a generation, the directors of labour and the distributors of food, peaceful Janissaries of the new order, would form themselves into a caste, very close, very coherent, and (unlike legislators for whom an executive council can always be substituted), quite indispensable, and would close their ranks round a chief who would give them unity and the strength of unity.

Before we knew socialism, we used to say that democracy tended naturally to despotism. The situation seems somewhat changed, and we might now say that it tends to socialism: really nothing has changed. For in tending towards socialism it is towards despotism that it tends. Socialism is not conscious of this, for it imagines that it is journeying towards equality, but out of these utopias of equality it is ever despotism that emerges.

But this is a digression which refers to the future; let us return to the matter in hand.

CHAPTER IV.
THE COMPETENT LEGISLATOR.

Democracy, in its modern form, encroaches first upon the executive and then upon the administrative authorities, and reduces them to subjection by means of its delegates, the legislators, whom it chooses in its own image, that is to say, because they are incompetent and governed by passion, just as in the words of Montesquieu, though he perhaps contradicts himself a little: "The people is moved only by its passions."

What ought then the character of the legislator to be? The very opposite, it seems to me, of the democratic legislator, for he ought to be well informed and entirely devoid of prejudice.

He ought to be well informed, but his information should not consist only of book learning, although an extensive legal knowledge is of the greatest use, as it will prevent him from doing, as so often happens, the exact opposite of what he intends to do. He should also understand intimately the temperament and character of the people for whom he legislates.

For a nation should only be given the laws and commandments that it can tolerate, as Solon said: "I have given them the best laws that they could endure," and the God of Israel said to the Jews: "I have given you precepts which are not good," that is to say, they have only the goodness which your wickedness will tolerate. "This is the sponge," says Montesquieu, "which wipes out all the difficulties that can be raised against the laws of Moses."

The legislator, then, ought to understand the temperament and genius of the people because he has to frame its laws. As the Germans say, he ought to be an expert on the psychology of races. Further, he ought to understand the temperament, peculiarities and character of the people, without sharing its temperament himself. For where the passions and inclinations are concerned, experience is not knowledge. On the contrary, experience prevents us from really knowing; and indeed one of the conditions of knowledge is absence of an experience which may be another word for bias.

The ideal legislator, or indeed any legislator worthy of the name, ought to understand the general tendencies of his people, but he ought to be able to view them from a position of detachment and to be able to control them, because it is his business partly to satisfy and partly to combat these tendencies.

He has partly to satisfy them, or at least, to consider them, because a law which outraged the national temperament would be like Roland's mare, which had every conceivable good quality with this one serious defect, that she was dead, and born dead. Suppose the Romans had been given an international law decreeing respect for conquered peoples, it would have been a dead letter, and by a sort of contagion it would have led to the neglect of other laws. Suppose the French were given a liberal law, a law prescribing respect for the individual rights of the man and the citizen. Liberty, the object of such a law, is for the French, as Baron Joannès has remarked: "The right of each man to do what he likes and to prevent other men from doing what they like." In France such a law would never obtain any but a very grudging allegiance, and it would certainly lead to the neglect of other laws.

The legislator ought therefore to understand the natural idiosyncrasies of his people in order to know how far he dare venture to oppose them.

Partly he must combat them, because law should be to a nation, or otherwise it is merely a police regulation, what the moral law is to an individual. Law should be a restraint imposed continuously in the hope of future improvements. It should be a curb on dangerous passions and injurious desires. It should aid the warfare of enlightened selfishness against the selfishness of which all are ashamed. That is what Montesquieu meant when he said that morals should correct climate, and laws should correct morals.

The law, therefore, to a certain extent should correct national tendencies, it should be loved a little because it is felt to be just, feared a little because it is severe, hated a little because it is to a certain degree out of sympathy with the prevalent temper of the day, and respected because it is felt to be necessary.

This is the law that the legislator has to frame, and therefore he ought to have expert knowledge of the genius of the people for whom he legislates. He must understand both those tendencies which will resist and those which will welcome him. He must know how far he can go unopposed and how much he can venture without forfeiting his authority.

This is the principal and essential qualification for the legislator.

The second, as we said before, is that he must be impartial. The very essence of the legislator is that he should have moderation, that virtue on which Cicero set so high a value, which is so rare, if we look to its real meaning, *the perfect balance of soul and mind.* "It seems to me," said Montesquieu: "*and I have written this book solely to prove it*, that the spirit of moderation is essential in a legislator, for political, as well as moral right, lies between two extremes."

Nothing is more difficult for a man than to control his passions, or more difficult for a legislator than to control the passions of the people of whom he forms a part, to say nothing of his own. "Aristotle," says Montesquieu, "wanted to gratify, first, his jealousy of Plato and then his love for Alexander. Plato was horrified at the tyranny of the Athenians. Machiavel was full of his idol, the Duke of Valentinois. Thomas More, who was wont to speak of what he had read rather than of what he had thought, wanted to govern every state upon the model of a Greek city. Harrington could think of nothing but an English republic, while hosts of writers thought confusion must reign wherever there was no monarchy. Laws are always in contact with the passions and prejudices of the legislator, whether these are his alone, or common to him and to his people. Sometimes they pass through and merely take colour from the prejudice of the day, sometimes they succumb to it and make it part of themselves."

This is just the opposite of what should be. The legislator should be to the people what conscience is to the heart of the individual. He should understand its besetting passions in all their bearings and not be deceived by subterfuge or hypocrisy. Sometimes he must attack them boldly, sometimes play off one against another, or favour one at the expense of another which is less influential, now yielding ground, now recovering it, but he must ever be skilful and impartial and never be intimidated, diverted from his purpose, nor deceived by his natural enemies.

He should be, so to speak, more conscientious than conscience itself, because he must never forget that he has to obey to-morrow the law which he makes to-day—*semel jussit semper paruit*. He must, therefore, be absolutely disinterested, a thing most difficult for him, but for which conscience requires no effort.

Not only must he be without passion, but he must have trained himself to be impervious to passion, which is much more. We must conceive of him as a conscience that has risen from the ashes of passion.

As Rousseau said, "to discover the perfect ruler for human society we must find a superior intelligence who has seen all the passions of man but has experienced none of them, who has had no sort of relations with our nature but who knows it to the core, whose happiness is not dependent on us, but who wishes to promote our welfare, in a word, one who aims at a distant renown, in a remote future, and[73] who is content to labour in one age and to enjoy in another."

This is why the ingenious Greeks imagined certain legislators going into exile to some remote and unknown retreat, as soon as they had made the people adopt and swear obedience to their laws until their return. It may have been to bind the citizens by this oath, but is it not equally probable that they wished to escape from the laws which they themselves had made? Possibly they felt that they could make them all the stricter with the prospect of being able to evade obedience of them by flight.

Proudhon said: "I dream of a republic so liberal that in it I shall be guillotined as a reactionary." Lycurgus was perhaps like Proudhon, in that he founded so severe a republic that he knew he could not live under it and resolved to leave it as soon as it was established. Solon and Sylla remained in the states to which they had given laws; we must therefore place them higher than Lycurgus who has perhaps this excuse for himself that in all probability he never existed at all.

But the legend remains to show that the legislator should be so superior to his own passions and to the passions of his people, that, as legislator, he should make laws before which, as a man, he should stand in awe.

This moderation, in the sense in which we use the term, has sometimes led the legislator to suggest or insinuate laws rather than impose them. This is not always possible, but it is so occasionally. Montesquieu tells us the following of St. Louis: "Seeing the manifold abuses of justice in his time he endeavoured to make them unpopular. He made many regulations for the courts in his own domain, and in those of his barons, and he was so successful, that only a short time after his death his methods were adopted in the courts by many of his nobles. Thus this prince attained his object, although his regulations were not promulgated as a general law for the whole kingdom, but merely as an example which any one might follow in his own interest. He got rid of an evil by making patent the better way. When men saw in his courts and in those of his nobles more reasonable and natural forms of procedure, more conformable to religion and morality, more favourable to public tranquillity and to the security of persons and property, they adopted the substance and abandoned the shadow. *To suggest where you cannot compel, to guide where you cannot demand, that is the supreme form of skill."*

Montesquieu adds with some optimism though no doubt the idea is encouraging: "Reason has a natural empire, we resist it, but it triumphs over our resistance; we persist in error for a time but we always have to return to it."

The instance above quoted is very remote, and can hardly be applied to anything in our day. But consider, for instance, the law of Sunday observance which has been revived from the ecclesiastical law. It was a mistake to include it in the Code because it was antagonistic to many French customs, and, in many ways, to the national temperament. The result is what might have been expected, namely, that it has only been carried out in rare instances, and with an infinity of trouble. It might have been made the subject of an edict without being included in the Code. The State might have given a holiday on Sunday to all its officials, employees and workmen. It might have been made quite clear simply by a circular from the Minister of Justice that a workman would not be punished for breach of contract by refusing to work on a Sunday. The law of a weekly day of rest would then have existed, without being formally promulgated, and would have been limited precisely where it should be, by agreement between masters and men who would submit to working on Sundays when they saw that it was necessary and inevitable. Moreover this law would be strong enough to modify without destroying the ancient customs of the people.

Here is another instance which occurs within the law laid down by the Code, where the legislator makes use of a method of suggestion and recommendation. Early in the nineteenth century the legislator considered that it was seemly for a husband who surprised his wife in adultery to kill both her and her accomplice. The sentiment is perhaps questionable, but at all events, it was current. Was it given legal sanction? No, not precisely. It is inserted in the law in the form of an insinuation, a discreet recommendation and affectionate encouragement. The legislator wrote these words: "In *flagrante delicto* murder is excusable." I am not approving the sentiment, but only this manner of indicating rather than enforcing the law and what is thought to be a wholesome practice, and in other instances I should think it excellent.

Finally, one of the essential qualities of the legislator is to show discretion in changing existing laws, and for this purpose he should be immune from the passions of men or at all events complete master of those which beset him. For law has no real authority unless it is ancient. Where a law is merely a custom which has become law, it is invested with considerable authority from the first, because it gains strength by the antiquity of the original custom. When on the other hand a law is not an old custom but runs counter to custom, then, before it can have any authority, it must grow old and become a custom itself.

In both cases it is on its antiquity that the law must depend for its strength. The law is like a tree, at first it is a tender sapling, then it grows up, its bark hardens, and its roots go deep into the ground and cling to the rock.

We ought to consider carefully before we venture to replace the forest tree by the young sapling. "Most legislators," said Usbek to Rhédi,[1] "have been men of limited abilities, owing their position to a stroke of fortune, and consulting nothing but their own whims and prejudices. They have often abolished established laws quite unnecessarily, and plunged nations into the chaos that is inseparable from change. It is true that, owing to some odd chance arising out of the nature rather than out of the intelligence of mankind, it is sometimes necessary to alter laws, but the case is very rare and when it does arise it should be handled with a reverent touch. When it is a question of changing the law, much ceremony should be observed, and many precautions taken, in order that the people may be naturally persuaded that laws are sacred things, and that many formalities must precede any attempt to alter them."

In this passage, as so often elsewhere, Montesquieu is quite Aristotelian, for Aristotle wrote: "It is evident that at times certain laws

---

[1] Characters in Montesquieu's *Lettres Persanes*. Letter cxxix.

must be changed, but this requires great circumspection for, when there is little to be gained thereby, inasmuch as it is dangerous that citizens should be accustomed to find it easy to change the law, it is better to leave a few errors in our magisterial and legislative arrangements than to accustom the people to constant change. The disadvantage of having constant changes in the law is greater than any risk that we run of contracting a habit of disobedience to the law." For the law assuredly will be disobeyed, if we regard it as ephemeral, unstable, and always on the point of being changed.

Some knowledge of the laws of the most important nations, a profound knowledge of the temperament, character, sentiments, passions, opinions, prejudices and customs of the nation to which he belongs, moderation of heart and mind, judgment, impartiality, coolness, nay even a measure of stolidity, these are the attributes of the ideal legislator. Rather they are the necessary qualifications of every man who purposes to frame a good law; they are, indeed, the elementary attributes of a legislator.

We have seen that it is the very opposite quality that democracy likes and expects of its legislators. It selects incompetent and almost invariably ignorant men, I have explained why;

and its nominees are of a double distilled incompetence in that their passions would certainly neutralise their efficiency if they possessed any.

Further we have to observe this curious fact. So entirely does democracy choose its legislators, because they are dominated by passion, and not in spite of the fact, chooses them indeed precisely for the reasons for which it ought to reject them, that any moderate, clear-headed, practical man who wants to be elected and make use of his powers, has to start by dissembling his moderation, and by making a noisy display of factious violence. If he wants to be nominated to a post where it will be his business to defend and guarantee public security, he has to begin by advocating civil war: to become a peacemaker he must first pose as a rebel.

Every popular favourite passes through these two phases, and has to complete one stage before he starts on the next. Is it not better, you will ask, that a man's whole career should be spent in defence of law and order rather than the latter part of it? Not at all, because you cannot exercise any influence as a friend of law and order unless you have begun as an anarchist.

These changes of opinion occur so frequently that they merely raise a smile. They have, however, this drawback, that the friend of law and order, with a seditious past, never has an undisputed authority, and he spends half his time explaining the reasons for his defection, and this is a sore let and hindrance to his subsequent career.

The people always elects men swayed by real or simulated passion. These will either always remain in a state of frenzied excitement, and they are the great majority, or they will become moderate men, largely disqualified and handicapped, as we have above shown, for their new career. The vast majority of these sentimentalists rush into politics instead of studying them with deliberation, judgment and wisdom. The canons of good government as above set out are entirely subverted. The law does not control and restrain the passions of the populace. Legislation becomes little more than an expression of their frenzy, a series of party measures levelled by one faction against the other. The introduction of a bill is a challenge; the passing of an act is a victory; definitions which at once damn the legislator, and convict the system.

CHAPTER V.
LAWS UNDER DEMOCRACY.

The truth of my contention is proved by the fact that nowadays all our laws are emergency laws, a thing that no law should ever be. Montesquieu advised people to be very chary and to think twice before they destroyed old laws or pulled down an old house to run up a tent, but his advice is completely ignored. New laws are made for every change in the weather, for every little daily incident in politics. We are getting used to this hand-to-mouth legislation. Like the barbarian warrior, of whom Demosthenes tells us, who always protected that portion of his person which had just received a blow, holding his shield up to his shoulder, when his shoulder had been struck, down again to his thigh when the blow fell there, the dominant faction only makes laws to protect itself against an adversary who is, or is thought to be, already in the field, or it introduces a hurried, ill-digested reform under the pressure of an alleged scandal.

If an aspirant to the tyranny, as they used to say in Athens, is nominated deputy in too many constituencies, instantly a law is passed prohibiting multiple candidatures. For the same reason, for fear of the same man, *scrutin de liste* is hurriedly replaced by *scrutin d'arrondissement.*[2]

---

[2] See *France*, by J. E. C. Bodley, 1899, pp. 334, 335. Under *Scrutin de liste* "the department is the electoral unit, each having its complement of deputies allotted to it in proportion to its population, and each elector having as many votes as there are seats ascribed to his

If an accused woman is supposed to have been ill-treated at her examination, taken too abruptly before the interrogatory of the president, or if the counts are ineptly set out by the public prosecutor, instantly the whole of the criminal procedure is radically reformed.

It is the same everywhere. The legislative workshops turn out only "the latest novelties" of the season. Or perhaps a newspaper would be a still better simile. First there is the 'interpellation,'[3] once at least every day; that corresponds to the leading article. Then there are questions for ministers on this, that and the other trivial occurrence; that is the serial or short story. Then there is a bill brought in about something that happened the night before, that is the special article. Then some deputy assaults his neighbour, this is the general news column.

---

department, without, however, the power to cumulate." *Scrutin d'arrondissement* is election by single-member constituencies.

The *arrondissement* is the electoral unit.

[3] This is a question put to a minister by a deputy. "The effect ... is somewhat similar to a motion to adjourn the house in the English Parliament." Bodley, p. 445.

You could not have a more faithful representation of the country. Everything that happens in the morning is dealt with in the evening as it might be in the village pot-house. The legislative chamber is an exaggerated reflection of the gossiping public. Now it ought not to be a copy of the country, it ought to be its soul and brain. But when a national representative assembly represents only the passions of the populace it cannot be otherwise than what it is.

In other words modern democracy *is not governed by laws* but by decrees, for emergency laws are no better than decrees. A law is an ancient heritage, consecrated by long usage, which men obey without stopping to think whether it be law or custom. It forms part of a coherent, harmonious and logical whole. A law improvised for an emergency is merely a decree. This is one of the things that Aristotle saw better than any one. He comments frequently upon the essential and fundamental distinction between the two, and explains how it is as dangerous to misunderstand as to ignore it. I quote the passage in which he brings this out most forcibly: "A fifth form of democracy is that in which not the law but the multitude has the supreme power, and supersedes the law by its decrees. This is a state of affairs brought about by the demagogues. For in democracies which are subject to the law, the best citizens hold the first place and there are no demagogues; but where the laws are not supreme, there demagogues spring up. For the people becomes a monarch and is many in one; and the many have the power in their hands, not as individuals but collectively.... And the people, who is now a monarch, and no longer under the control of law, seeks to exercise monarchical sway, and grows into a despot; the flatterer is held in honour; this sort of democracy being relatively to other democracies what tyranny is to other forms of monarchy.

"The spirit of both is the same, and they alike exercise a despotic rule over the better citizens. The decrees of the Demos correspond to the edicts of the tyrant, and the demagogue is to the one what the flatterer is to the other. Both have great power—the flatterer with the tyrant, the demagogue with democracies of the kind which we are describing. The demagogues make the decrees of the people override the laws, and refer all things to the popular assembly. And therefore they grow great, because the people has all things in its hands and they hold in their hands the votes of the people, who is too ready to listen to them. Such a democracy is fairly open to the objection that it is not a constitution at all; for *where the laws have no authority there is no constitution.* The law ought to be supreme over all. So that if democracy be a real form of government, *the sort of constitution in which all things are regulated by decrees is clearly not a democracy in the true sense of the word,* for decrees relate only to particulars."

This distinction between true law, that is to say, venerable law, framed to endure, part of a co-ordinate scheme of legislation, and an emergency law which is merely a decree like the wishes of a tyrant, constitutes the whole difference, if we could realise it, between the sociologists of antiquity and those of to-day. By the term Law, the ancient and the modern sociologists mean two different things and this is the reason for so many misunderstandings. When he speaks of law, the modern sociologist means the expression of the general will at such and such a date, 1910 for instance. The ancient sociologist would consider that the expression of the general will in the second year of the 73rd Olympiad was not law at all, but a decree. A law to him would be a paragraph of the legislation of Solon, Lycurgus or Charondas. Whenever in a Greek or Roman political treatise we meet the expression—"a State governed by laws," the only way to translate it is—"a State governed by a very ancient and immutable legislation." This gives the true meaning to the famous personification of laws in the Phædo, which would be quite meaningless if the Greeks had understood what we do by the term. Are laws the expression of the general will of the people? If so why should Socrates have respected them, he who despised the people to the day he was condemned? It would be absurd. These laws which Socrates respected were not the decrees of the people contemporary with Socrates; they were the ancient gods of the city, which had protected it from the earliest days.

These laws may err in that they seemed to sanction the verdict that condemned Socrates to death, but they were honourable, venerable and inviolate, because they had been the guardians of the city for centuries, and guardians of Socrates himself until the day when they were misapplied against him.

A "constitution," therefore, to adopt Aristotle's terminology, is a State which obeys laws, that is to say, laws framed by its ancestors.

It is, then, an aristocracy, for it is even more aristocratic to obey our ancestors themselves by obeying the thoughts which they embedded in legislation, five centuries ago, than to obey the inheritors of their tradition, the aristocrats of to-day. For aristocrats of to-day belong only partly to tradition, in that they live in the present. Whereas a fifteenth century law belongs to the fifteenth century and to no other period. To obey law as understood by the ancient sociologists, did not mean obeying Scipio who has just passed us on the *Via Sacra*. It meant to obey his grandfather's great grandfather! All this is ultra-aristocratic.

Precisely! *Law is an aristocratic thing;* only *the emergency law*, the *decree*, is democratic. For this reason Montesquieu always speaks of a monarchy as being limited, and, at the same time, maintained by its law. What did this mean in his day, when there was no "expression of the general will" to limit monarchy, and when royalty possessed legislative power, and could at will make and remake laws? It could only mean one thing, namely, that Montesquieu's conception of law was the same as that of the ancient sociologists,—law far older than his time, "fundamental laws" as he calls them, of the ancient monarchy, which still bind and ought so to bind the monarch, whose rule without them would be despotism or anarchy. Law is essentially aristocratic. It ordains that rulers should govern the people, and that the dead should govern the rulers. The very essence of aristocracy is the rule of those who have lived over those who live, for the benefit of those who shall live hereafter. Aristocracy, properly so called, is an aristocracy in the flesh. Law is a spiritual aristocracy. Aristocracy, as represented by the aristocrats of to-day, only represents the dead by tradition, inheritance, education, physiological heredity of temperament and characteristics. Law does not represent the dead, it is the dead themselves, it is their very thought perpetuated in immutable script.

A nation is aristocratic both in form and spirit which preserves its old aristocracy and maintains its vitality by careful infusions of new blood. Still more is that nation aristocratic which maintains its old legislation inviolate, adding to it, reverently and discreetly, new laws which combine something of the modern spirit with the spirit of the old. *Homines novi, novæ res. Homo novus* means the man without ancestors who is worthy to be added to the ranks of the nobly born. *Novæ res* are things without antecedents, nay revolution itself. *Novæ res* should only be introduced partially gradually, insensibly and progressively into ancient things, as "new men" into the community of the old nobility. Law is more aristocratic than aristocracy itself, hence democracy is the natural enemy of laws and can only tolerate decrees.

Our examination of modern democracy has brought us to the following conclusions. The representation of the country is reserved for the incompetent and also for those biassed by passion, who are doubly incompetent. The representatives of the people want to do everything themselves. They do everything badly and infect the government and the administration with their passion and incompetence.

CHAPTER VI.

THE INCOMPETENCE OF GOVERNMENT.

This is not all. The law of incompetence spreads still further, either by some process of logical necessity or by a sort of contagion. It has often been made the subject of merriment, for, like all tragedy, when we regard it with good humour the matter has its comic side, that it is very rare for any high office to be given to a man who is competent for the post. Generally the Minister of Education is a lawyer; the Minister of Commerce, an author; the War Minister, a doctor; the Minister for the Navy, a journalist. Beaumarchais' epigram "The post required a mathematician—it was given to a dancing master!" strikes the keynote much more of a democracy than of an absolute monarchy.

The matter is so generally recognised that it has a sort of retroactive effect upon the historical ideas of the masses. Three Frenchmen out of every four are convinced that Carnot was a civilian, and the statement has often appeared in print. Why? because it is inconceivable that under a democracy the War Minister could possibly be a soldier, or, that the members of the Convention could possibly have given the War Office to a soldier. This appeared too paradoxical to be true.

At first sight this extraordinary method of making incompetent men into ministers seems merely a joke, merely the subtle and entertaining vagaries of the goddess Incompetence. Partly it is so but not entirely. The man whose business it is to appoint ministers has to divide the choicest plums of office among the various groups of the majority which supports him. As all of these groups do not contain specialists, the highest offices are disposed of on political grounds, and not on grounds of professional aptitude. I have shown what the result is; the only ministerial appointment which is made in a rational manner is that which the President of the Council reserves for himself, and even in this case in order to conciliate some important political personage he very often gives it up and takes some post for which he is not so well suited.

See what follows: each department is directed by an incompetent man, who, if he be conscientious, sets himself to learn the work in which he ought to be a fully trained expert, or, if he be not conscientious, and be pressed for time, as he always is, he directs his department according to his general political theories and not according to practical common sense—a double distillation of incompetence.

We know the kind of speech a new Minister of Agriculture makes to his staff. He harangues them on the principles of the revolution of 1789.

Moreover, in a highly centralised country, the minister does everything in his own department. He has to do everything under the pressure, it is true, of the national representatives; but still his is the supreme authority. It is easy to see what sort of decisions he will make. They are often very little supported by law, and sometimes are even contrary to law, and then they remain a dead letter from the first. Ministerial circulars often have a remarkable character for illegality. In that case they fall and are forgotten, but [95] not always before they have introduced a vast amount of trouble throughout the entire administration.

As to appointments, they are made, as I have said, by political influence, and even when they are flagrantly improper and corrupt, there is no chance of their being corrected by the competence of a minister, who, holding enlightened views on the business and subordinates of his office, is able to put his foot down and say "No! this will not do, we must draw the line somewhere."

CHAPTER VII.
JUDICIAL INCOMPETENCE.

Here we find incompetence spreading its influence by the logical necessity of the case. There are other quarters in which it grows by a sort of contagion. Have you ever noticed that the *ancien régime*, in spite of grievous shortcomings, by a sort of historical tradition, maintained a certain respect for efficiency in its different forms? For instance in matters of jurisdiction, there were seignorial, ecclesiastical and military courts. These were not founded as the result of argument and profound consideration, but by the natural course of events, by history itself, and they were maintained and approved by a monarchy which was verging on despotism.

Seignorial jurisdiction, without much rational justification, was none the less of considerable utility; it bound, or was capable of binding, the noble to his land, it prevented him from losing sight of his vassals, and his vassals from losing sight of him, and was in fact a conservative force in the aristocratic constitution of the kingdom. I submit that if this jurisdiction had been properly defined, limited and modified, which was never done, it would have been consonant with the law of competence. There are various local matters which come quite properly within the province of the noble, who in those days took the place of the magistrate. All that was wanted was that such matters should have been defined with precision and that in every case appeal should have been allowed.

Ecclesiastical jurisdiction was perfectly reasonable, as offences committed by ecclesiastics have a special character of which ecclesiastics alone can judge. This seems strange to modern ideas, although nowadays there are commercial courts and conciliation boards, because litigation between men of business, between workmen and women workers, and between employers and employed, can only be decided by men who have technical knowledge of the subject in dispute. Appeal, moreover, to a higher court is always allowed.

Finally, in the old days there used to be military jurisdiction for precisely the same reason.

All these exceptional jurisdictions are objects of the liveliest apprehension to democracy, because they infringe the rule of uniformity, which is the image and often the caricature of equality, and also because they are a stronghold of efficiency.

Democracy of course demolished aristocratic courts together with the aristocracy itself, and ecclesiastical courts together with the Church when it ceased to be an estate of the realm. Any special jurisdictions which still remain are looked upon as instruments of aristocracy; courts-martial are held in abhorrence because they have ideas of their own in respect of military honour and duty, and military offences. Therein lies their efficiency, a thing absolutely necessary, if we are to maintain military spirit and discipline in a strong army. The private soldier or officer, who is only judged and punished as a civilian, will not be well judged nor adequately punished, considering the special duties and services which are required of the army. This is a question of moral as well as technical efficiency and to this the democracy pays no heed, because it is convinced that no special efficiency is necessary and that common sense is all that is required. Common sense, however, is like wit; it is useful in every walk of life, but is not sufficient in any one of them. This is just what democracy cannot or will not understand.

It makes just as great a mistake in its civil and criminal jurisdiction, though it has, up to now, so far departed from its principles as to appoint qualified jurists to civil judgeships. No one denies that this body of men is efficient. Those who act as judges know their law. There is, however, as I have often had occasion to point out, a moral as well as a technical efficiency, and in limiting the independence that is essential to moral efficiency, democracy neutralises the technical efficiency of its servants. Let me explain my meaning further.

Formerly the magistracy was a recognised and autonomous branch of the public service, and as a result, save as it was affected by revolution and in normal times by the fear of revolution, enjoyed an absolute independence. This gave, or rather preserved intact, its moral efficiency. For moral efficiency consists in an ability to act according to the dictates of conscience, and is equivalent to a sort of moral independence.

Now, the magistrates form a department of the administration and are a body of officials. The State appoints, promotes or refuses to promote and pays them. In short the State has them at its mercy, just as military officers are controlled by the War Office, or tax-collectors by the Treasury. Hence they are deprived of their independence and moral efficiency, for they are always tempted to give judgment as the Government would wish.

There is, it is true, a guarantee for their independence in the permanence of their appointments, but this only applies to those who have reached the summit of their profession, or are on the point of retiring, or have no further interest in promotion. The young magistrate who wants to get on, a perfectly legitimate ambition, is by no means independent, for if he does not give satisfaction, he may enjoy a peculiar kind of permanence, the permanence of standing still at the starting point. The only independent judges, to whom justice is the sole interest, are either those who have served for forty years or the President of the *Cour de Cassation*. I may add also the man of independent means who is indifferent to promotion and content to spend all his time at the place of his first appointment. He is exactly like the magistrates in old days, but he and his kind get rarer every year.

At best, moreover, this permanence, of which so much is thought, is an illusory guarantee, for it is often suspended by one Government or another, and the magistrates are constantly at the mercy of political crises. Their moral efficiency is indeed sorely tried.

I affirm, therefore, that this diminution of moral efficiency affects technical efficiency, because magistrates dare not insist on technical exactitude when cases arise between the State and individuals, or between those who are protected by Government and those who are not. Though cases in which the State is a party do not occur very often, those in which friends of the Government are involved are of daily occurrence in a country where Government is a faction waging incessant warfare against all other factions.

It has been said with much reason that parliamentary government on a basis of universal suffrage is legalised and continuous civil war. It is usually a bloodless civil war, but its weapons are insults, provocations, calumnies, personalities, libel actions. These go on from one year's end to the other. In a country where such a state of affairs is prevalent, the magistracy ought to be absolutely independent in order to be impartial. Yet it is precisely in a country like this that the magistracy, not being independent and autonomous, is obliged to avoid offending the party in office which, moreover, is extremely exacting, for it lives in constant fear that it may be turned out of power.

—Is there nothing to be done? Would you advocate a return to the practice of purchasing judicial appointments?—

In the first place, this would not be anything so very terrible, and secondly, it might be quite possible to secure all the advantages of purchase without its actual practice.

I can show you that it is not so very terrible, for the case is parallel with that of the exceptional jurisdictions, the mention of which filled you with horror till you remembered the commercial courts and the councils of experts, all excellent institutions. We are appalled at the idea of a magistrate purchasing his office, and yet we employ advocates and solicitors and other legal officials and trust them with our most precious interests, yet they have, many of them, either bought or inherited their practice. Under a system of purchase, we should be judged by lawyers of whom we required more extensive legal knowledge than is at present required of the profession. We should be judged in fact by solicitors and advocates of a superior order. There is nothing very alarming about that.

Montesquieu was in favour of a system of purchase. Voltaire opposed it strongly. They were both right and were indeed agreed on general principles. Montesquieu says: "Venality,—the purchase system,—is a good thing under a monarchical form of government, because work which would not be done from mere civic virtue is then undertaken as a family business. Each man's duty is laid down for him, and the orders of the State are given greater permanence. Suidas says very aptly of Anastasius that he turned the Empire into an aristocracy by selling magisterial offices."

Voltaire replies: "Is it as a matter of civic virtue that in England a judge of the King's Bench accepts his appointment?" (It is either a matter of civic virtue or of profit and interest, and if it is not profit, it certainly must require considerable civic virtue.) "What! can we not find men in France willing to judge if we bestow their appointments upon them gratuitously?" (We certainly can: but they might be too grateful!) "Can the work of administering justice, disposing of the lives and fortunes of men, become a family business?" (Well, the business of bearing arms and disposing of men's lives and fortunes in civil war was in 1760 a family business. So too the business of being king, and you do not protest against that!) "It is a pity that Montesquieu should dishonour his work by such paradoxes, but we must forgive him; his uncle purchased a provincial magistrate's office and left it to him. Human nature comes in everywhere. None of us is without weaknesses."

Montesquieu thinks aristocratic bodies are good things. Voltaire is in favour of absolute power. Montesquieu would like the judicature to be a family office, that is to say hereditary like the profession of a soldier; this would make the judicial profession permanent like other professions. He demonstrates, as does Suidas, that the purchase system creates an aristocracy. Voltaire, like Napoleon I., would make his soldiers, his priests, and his judges, king's men. They should all belong to the king, body and soul.

Montesquieu had a greater antagonist than Voltaire in Plato. Plato wrote in his Republic, referring to all judicial offices: "It is as if on board ship a man were made a pilot for his wealth. Can it be that such a rule is bad in every other calling, and good only in respect of the governing of a republic?"

Montesquieu answers Plato (and in anticipation Voltaire) very wittily: "Plato is speaking of a virtuous republic and I of a mere monarchy. Under a monarchy if offices were not sold by rule, the poverty and greed of courtiers would sell them all the same, and chance after all will give a better result than the choice of a prince."

To sum up, Montesquieu wants the magistracy to be partly hereditary, and partly recruited from the wealthy classes, an independent, aristocratic body analogous to the army or the clergy, administering justice with that technical efficiency which university standards can guarantee, and with the moral efficiency which is founded on independence, dignity, public spirit and impartiality.

I said above that venality, or the system of purchase, was not necessary to obtain these results. The principle is this, that the magistracy must be independent, and to be independent it must have a proprietary right in its duties. This can only be obtained if it hold its office by inheritance or purchase as was done under the *ancien régime*; or, if it were somehow contrived that magistrates should not be chosen by the Government. The purchase or inheritance plan is not popular, then the only alternative is that the magistrates should be chosen by some body other than the Government. By whom then? The people? Then the judges would be dependent upon the people and the electors.

—That would be better, or less bad.—

Not at all. If the judges were chosen by the electors, they would be even less impartial than if they were elected by the Government. The judge then would think of nothing but of being re-elected. He would always give judgment in favour of the party which had elected him. Would you care to be judged before a court composed of the deputies of your department? Certainly not, if you belong to the weaker party. Yes, if you belong to the majority, but then only if you are certain that your adversary belongs to the minority, or, if he belong to your own party, that he is a less influential elector than yourself. To sum up, there is no guarantee of impartiality if the judges are elected.

Further, if the system of electing judges by those liable to their jurisdiction were adopted, there would be an extensive and, I might add, a most entertaining variety of justice. Judges, who were elected by a "blue" or republican majority, and who were anxious for re-election, would always deliver judgment in favour of the blues. The same thing would happen in the "white" or royalists districts. "Justice has her epochs," Pascal said ironically, and in this case justice would have her districts. It would not be the same in the *Alpes-Maritimes* as in the *Côtes-du-Nord*. The Court of Appeal, if it attempted to be impartial, would spend its time sending cases back from a blue district to be revised in a white, and the decisions delivered in a white country to be revised in a blue. There would be judicial and legal anarchy.

—If the bench is not to be inherited, nor bought, nor chosen by the Government, nor elected by the people, by whom is it to be nominated?—

By itself; I see no other solution.

For instance I can suggest one good method, though there may be several. All the doctors of law in France could choose the judges of appeal and the judges of appeal could choose and promote all the judges. This is an aristocratic-democratic scheme on a very broad basis.

Or else the judges alone might choose the judges of appeal, and the judges of appeal might appoint and promote the judges. That is an oligarchical method.

Or again, here is a plan for passing from the system that is, to that which ought to be. For the first time the doctors of law might choose the *Cour de Cassation*, and it could choose the judges. Afterwards the judges could fill the vacancies in the *Cour de Cassation*, which would nominate and promote the judges.

The Government would still go on, and continue to nominate the persons eligible to serve as magistrates.

Under all these systems the judges would form an autonomous, self-creative body, dependent upon and responsible to themselves alone, and by reason of their absolute independence, strictly impartial.

—But they would form a caste!—

They would form a caste. I am sorry for it, but it is the case. You will never be well judged until you have a judicial caste, which is neither the Government, nor the world at large. For the Government cannot judge properly when it is both judge and party to the suit. Further, if it be litigious; it will never be out of court. Again, the world at large cannot judge properly, because, in practice, the world at large means the majority, and the majority is a party, and by definition a party can hardly be impartial.

But democracy does not want to be judged by a caste. In the first place because it abhors castes, and secondly because it does not care about impartial justice. Do not exclaim at the paradox. Democracy does want to be judged impartially in little every-day cases, but in all important cases in which a political question is involved and in which one of the majority is opposed to one of the minority, the verdict then has to be for the stronger side.

It says to the judicial bench what a simple-minded deputy said to the President of the Chamber: "It is your duty to protect the majority."

This is why democracy clings to its official magistracy, which contains some good elements though its members cannot always be impartial. They were condemned by the mouth of one of their highest dignitaries who answered when questioned about some illegal proceeding: "There are reasons of high State policy," thus throwing both the law and the judges at the feet of the Government. On another occasion, with the very best intentions, in order to put an end to an interminable affair, they turned and twisted the law and set a bad example; for by not applying the law correctly, they laid themselves open to endless and justifiable attacks upon their decision; they did not procure the longed-for settlement, and, instead, left the matter open to interminable dispute. They have knowledge, good sense and intelligence, but as their want of independence, in other words their moral inefficiency, neutralises their technical efficiency, they do not and cannot possess authority.

Democracy will inevitably go further along the road towards its ideal, which is direct government. It will want to elect the judges.

Already it chooses them remotely in the third degree; for it chooses the deputies who choose the Government, which chooses the judges; and to some extent, in the second degree, for it chooses the deputies who bring pressure to bear upon the nomination of the judges and interfere with their promotion and their decisions. This also is remote.

And, as by this constitution, or, rather by this practice, recognition is given to the principle that it is the people who really appoints the judges through its intermediaries, democracy, always logical and matter of fact, would like to see the principle applied without concealment, and the people making the appointments directly.

Then endless questions will arise about the best way of voting and electing. If unipersonal ballot is adopted, the canton will nominate its *juge de paix*, the district its tribunal, the region its Court, and the whole country the Court of Appeal. In this arrangement there will be the double drawback mentioned above; that is, varying interpretations of justice according to districts, and no impartiality.

If, on the other hand, *scrutin de liste* is adopted, the whole country will choose all the magistrates and they will belong to the majority. In this case there would be uniformity of justice but no impartiality. Any intermediate system would combine the disadvantage of both plans. For instance, if nominations are made in each division, all the magistrates in Brittany will be white partisans, while in Provence they will be blue partisans. In both cases they will be biassed, and such diversity as there is will be merely a diversity of partiality and bias.

We are talking of the future, though not perhaps of a very distant one. Let us deal with the present. The jury is still with us. Now the jury combines absolute moral competence with absolute technical incompetence. Democracy must always have incompetence in one form or another. A jury is independent of everybody, both of the Government and of the people, and in the best possible way, because it is the agent of the people without being elected. It does not seek re-election and is rather vexed than otherwise at being summoned to perform a disagreeable duty. On the other hand it always vacillates between two emotions, between pity and self-preservation, between feelings of humanity and the necessity for social protection; it is equally sensitive to the eloquence of the defending advocate, and the summing up of the prosecutor, and as these two influences balance each other it is in a perfect moral condition for delivering an equitable verdict.

For this reason the jury is of ancient origin, and has always been an institution in the land. At Athens the tribunal of the Heliasts formed a kind of jury, too numerous indeed and more like a public meeting, but still a sort of jury.

At Rome, a better regulated republic, there were certain citizens chosen by the prætor who settled questions of fact, that is to say, decided whether an act had or had not been committed, whether a sum of money had or had not been paid; and the question of law was reserved for the centumvirs.

In England the jury still exists and has existed for centuries.

These various peoples have considered very properly that juries are excellently adapted for forming equitable decisions, since they possess a greater moral competence for this particular function, than is to be found elsewhere.

This is true; but on the other hand a jury has no intelligence. In November 1909, a jury in the Côte d'Or before whom a murderer was being tried, declared (1) that this man did not strike the blows, (2) that the blows which he struck resulted in death. Thereupon the man was acquitted, although his violence, which never took place, had a murderous result.

In the Steinheil case in the same month and year, the jury's verdict involved (1) that no one had been assassinated in the Steinheils' house, and (2) that Mme Steinheil was not the daughter of Mme Japy. If a verdict were a judgment this would have put an end to all attempts to discover the assassins of M. Steinheil and Mme Japy, and on the other hand there would have been terrible social complications.

But the verdict of a jury is not a judgment. Why? Because the legislator foresaw the alarming absurdity of verdicts. It is presumed in law that all juries' verdicts are absurd, and experience proves that this is often the case. Juries' verdicts always seem to have been decided by lot like those of the famous judge in Rabelais, and it is proverbial at the law courts that it is impossible to foresee the issue of any case that comes before a jury. It looks as if the jury reasoned thus: "I am a chance judge, and it is only right that my judgment should be dictated by chance."

Voltaire was in favour of the jury system, principally because he had such a very low opinion of the magistrates of his day, whom he used to compare to Busiris. But, with his usual inconsequence, he takes no pains to conceal the fact that the populations of Abbeville and its neighbourhood were unanimously exasperated against La Barre and D'Etalonde, and the people of Toulouse against Calas, and all of them would have been condemned by juries summoned from those districts as surely as they were by the magisterial Busiris.

The jury system is nothing but a refined example of the cult of incompetence. Society, having to defend itself against thieves and murderers, lays the duty of defending it on some of its citizens, and arms them with the weapon of the law. Unfortunately it chooses for the purpose citizens who do not know how to use the weapon. It then fondly imagines that it is adequately protected. The jury is like an unskilled gladiator entangled in the meshes of his own net.

I need hardly say that democracy with its usual pertinacity is now trying to reduce the jury a step lower, and draw it from the lower instead of the lower middle classes. I see no harm in this myself, for in the matter of law the ignorance and inexperience of the lower middle class and the ignorance of the working class are much the same. I have only mentioned it to show the tendency of democracy towards what is presumably greater incompetence.

Now comes the turn of the *juges de paix*. At present we still have *juges de paix*. Here we have a most interesting example of the way democracy strives after incompetence in matters judicial.

Owing to the expense entailed by an appeal the jurisdiction of a *juge de paix* is very often final. He ought to be an instructed person with some knowledge of law and jurisprudence. He is therefore usually chosen from men who have a degree in law or from lawyers' clerks who have a certificate of ability. To be quite honest this is but a feeble guarantee.

By the law of July 12th, 1905, the French Senate, anxious to find men of still grosser incompetence, decided that *juges de paix* might be nominated from those, who, not having the required degree or certificate, had occupied the posts of mayor, deputy-mayor or councillor for ten years.

The object of this decision was the very honest and legitimate one of giving senators and deputies the opportunity of rewarding the electoral services of the village mayors and their assistants. And remember senators especially are nominated by these officials. Further it was an opportunity not to be missed for applying our principle—and our principle is this: we ask, where is absolute incompetence to be found, for to him who can lay indisputable claim to it we must confide authority.

Now mayors and their assistants answer this description exactly. They must be able to sign their names, but they are not obliged to know how to read, and eighty per cent. of them are totally illiterate. Their work is done for them very usually by the local schoolmaster. The Senate, therefore, was quite sure of finding among them men absolutely incompetent for the post of *juge de paix*, and it has found what it wanted. Incompetence so colossal deserved an appointment, and an appointment has been given to it.

The magistrature and the powers that be, seem to have been somewhat disturbed by certain consequences of this highly democratic institution. M. Barthou, the Minister of Justice, complained bitterly of the work which this new institution caused him. He made the following speech in the Chamber of Deputies: "We are here to tell each other the truth, and, with all the due moderation and prudence that is fitting, I feel it my duty to warn the chamber against the results of the law of 1905. At the present moment I am besieged with applications for the post of *juge de paix*. I need hardly mention that there are some 9,000 of them in my office, because a certain number are not eligible for consideration, but there are in round numbers 5,500 applications which are recommended and examined." (What he means to say is, that these are examined because they have been recommended, for, as is only right, those that are not backed by some political personage are not looked at.) "As the average annual number of vacancies is a hundred and eighty, you will readily see what a quandary I am in. Some of these applications are made with the most extraordinary persistency, I might even call it ferocity, and these invariably come from men who have held the office of mayor or deputy-mayor for ten years, often in the most insignificant places."

The Minister of Justice then read a report made on the subject by a *procureur-général*.

"In this department there are forty-seven *juges de paix*, twenty of whom, as I learn from an enquiry, were mayors at the time of their appointment. It is not to be wondered at that the number of provincial magnates who aspire to the post is on the increase, for it seems to be generally recognised in this department that elective office irrespective of all professional aptitude is the normal means of access to a paid appointment, more especially to that of *juge de paix*. Once they are appointed, the mayors combine both their municipal and judicial duties, and their interests lie far more in the commune which they administer than in the district in which they dispense justice and which, without permission, they should never leave. Sometimes these district magistrates will go to any length to obtain moral support from the politicians of the neighbourhood. They extort this as a sort of blackmail given in exchange for the electoral influence which they can bring to bear in their municipal capacity. They attach far less importance to being quashed by the bench, than to the eventual support of the deputy. Those who come into their courts are the unfortunate victims of these compromising arrangements which are giving the Republican system a bad name."

I think the Minister of Justice and his *procureur-général* have very little ground for these lamentations. After all the minister only complains of having 9,000 applications for office. It would surely be quite easy for him, in compliance with the generally recognised principle, to choose those whose incompetence seems to be most thorough, or those who are most influentially supported, according to the prevailing custom.

As for the *procureur-général's* sarcasms, which he thinks so witty, they are quite delightfully diverting and ingenuous. "It seems to be generally recognised that elective office, irrespective of all professional aptitude, is the normal means of access to a paid appointment." What else does he expect? It is eminently democratic that the marked absence of professional capacity should single a man out for employment. That is the very spirit of democracy. He surely does not think that a man is an elector by reason of his legislative and administrative capacity?

It is likewise essentially democratic that elective office should lead to paid appointments, for the democratic theory is that all office, paid and unpaid, should be elective. Why, this *procureur-général* must be an aristocrat!

As for the mutual services rendered by the justice, as mayor, to the deputy, and by the deputy to the justice, this is democracy pure and simple. The deputies distribute favours that they may be returned to power; the influential electors put all their interest, both personal and official, at the service of the deputies in order to obtain those favours. They are hand in glove with each other, and form a solid union of interests.

What more does the *procureur-général* want? Does he want a different system? If he wants another system, whatever else it may be, it will not be democracy, or at least it will not be a democratic democracy. Nor have I any idea what he means when he says the Republican system will get a bad name. The good name of the Republic depends upon its putting into practice every democratic principle; and democratic principles have certainly never been more precisely realised than in the preceding example, which I have had great pleasure in rescuing from oblivion and presenting to the notice of sociologists.

CHAPTER VIII.
EXAMPLES OF
INCOMPETENCE.

I have already compared this, our desire to worship incompetence, to an infectious disease. It has attacked the State at the very core, in its constitution, and it is not surprising that it is spreading rapidly to the customs and to the morals of the country.

The stage, we know, is an imitation of life. Life also, to perhaps an even greater extent, is an imitation of the stage. Similarly laws spring from morals, and morals spring from law. "Men are governed by many things," said Montesquieu, "by climate, religion, laws, precept, example, morals and manners, which act and react upon each other and all combine to form a general temperament."

Morals, more often than not, determine the nature of our laws, particularly in a democracy, which is deplorable, but Montesquieu was right in saying: "Morals take their colour from laws, and manners from morals," for laws certainly "help to form morals, manners" and even "national character." For instance in Rome under the Empire the code of morals was to some extent the result of arbitrary power, as to-day the moral character of the English is to some extent due to the laws and constitution of their country.

We know that by his laws Peter the Great changed if not the character at least the manners and customs of his people.

Custom is the offspring of law, and morals are the offspring of custom. National character is not really changed, for character, I believe, is a thing incapable of change, but it appears to be changed, and it certainly undergoes some modifications; one set of tendencies is checked, while others are encouraged.

The law abolishing the right of primogeniture has obviously affected national morals, though it has not otherwise altered national character. For a peculiar mental attitude is evolved by the constant domination of an elder brother, whose birthright gives him precedence and authority second only to that of the father. In countries where the right of unrestricted testamentary bequests is still maintained, family morals are very different from those which obtain where the child is considered a joint proprietor of the patrimony.

Since the passing of the law permitting divorce, a sad but necessary evil, there have been far more applications for divorce than there ever were for separation. Can this be accounted for solely by the fact that formerly it seemed hardly worth while to take steps to obtain the qualified freedom of separation? I think not. For when a yoke is unbearable, efforts to relax it would naturally be quite as strenuous and as unremitting as efforts to get rid of it altogether.

The truth is, I think, that when both civil and ecclesiastical law agreed in prohibiting divorce, people held a different view of marriage; it was looked upon as something sacred, as a tie that it was shameful to break, and that could not be broken except as a last resource and then almost under pain of death. The law permitting divorce was what our forefathers would have called a "legal indiscretion." It has abolished the feeling of shame. Except where there is strong religious feeling, there is now no scruple nor shame in seeking divorce. The old order has passed away; modesty has been superseded by a desire for liberty, or for another union. This change has been brought about by a law which was the result of a new moral code; but the law itself has helped to enlarge and expand the code.

Thus democracy extends that love of incompetence which is its most imperious characteristic. Greek philosophers used to delight in imagining what morals, especially domestic morals, would be like under a democracy. They all vied with Aristophanes. One of Xenophon's characters says: "I am pleased with myself, because I am poor. When I was rich I had to pay court to my calumniators, who knew full well that they could harm me more than I could them. Then the Republic was always imposing fresh taxes and I could not escape. Now that I am poor, I am invested with authority; no one threatens me. I threaten others. I am free to come and go as I choose. The rich rise at my approach and give me place. I was a slave, now I am a king; I used to pay tribute, now the State feeds me. I no longer fear misfortunes, and I hope to acquire wealth."

Plato too is quietly humorous at democracy's expense. "This form of government certainly seems the most beautiful of all, and the great variety of types has an excellent effect. At first sight does it not appear a privilege most delightful and convenient that we cannot be forced to accept any public office however eligible we may be, that we need not submit to authority and that every one of us can become a judge or magistrate as our fancy dictates? Is there not something delightful in the benevolence shown to criminals? Have you ever noticed how, in such a State as this, men condemned to death or exile remain in the country and walk abroad with the demeanour of heroes? See with what condescension and tolerance democrats despise the maxims which we have been brought up from childhood to revere and associate with the welfare of the Republic. We believe that unless a man is born virtuous, he will never acquire virtue, unless he has always lived in an environment of honesty and probity and given it his earnest attention. See with what contempt democrats trample these doctrines under foot and never stop to ask what training a man has had for public office. On the contrary, anyone who merely professes zeal in the public interests is welcomed with open arms. It is instantly assumed that he is quite disinterested.

"These are only a few of the many advantages of democracy. It is a pleasant form of government *in which equality reigns among unequal as well as among equal things.* Moreover, when a democratic State, athirst for liberty, is controlled by unprincipled cupbearers, who give it to drink of the pure wine of liberty and allow it to drink till it is drunken, then if its rulers do not show themselves complaisant and allow it to drink its fill, they are accused and overthrown under the pretext that they are traitors aspiring to an oligarchy; for the people prides itself on and loves the equality that confuses and will not distinguish between those who should rule and those who should obey. Is it any wonder that the spirit of licence, insubordination, and anarchy should invade everything, even the institution of the family? Fathers learn to treat their children as equals and are half afraid of them, while children neither fear nor respect their parents. All the citizens and residents and even strangers aspire to equal rights of citizenship.

"Masters stand in awe of their disciples and treat them with the greatest consideration and are jeered at for their pains. Young men want to be on the same terms as their elders and betters, and old men ape the manners of the young, for fear of being thought morose and dictatorial. Observe too to what lengths of liberty and equality the relations between the sexes are carried. You would hardly believe how much freer domestic animals are there than elsewhere. It is proverbial that little lap-dogs are on the same footing as their mistresses, or as horses and asses; they walk about with their noses in the air and get out of nobody's way."

Aristotle, faithless at this point to his favourite method of always contradicting Plato, has no particular liking, as we have said, for democracy. He does not spare it though he does not imitate Plato's scathing sarcasm.

In the first place, Aristotle is frankly in favour of slavery, as was every ancient philosopher except perhaps Seneca; but he is more insistent on this point than anyone else, for he looks upon slavery, not as one of many foundations, but as the very foundation of society.

He considers artisans as belonging to a higher estate but still as a class of "half-slaves." He asserts as an historical fact that only extreme and decadent democracies gave them rights of citizenship, and theoretically he maintains that no sound government would give them the franchise of the city. "Hence in ancient times, and among some nations, the working classes had no share in the government—a privilege which they only acquired under the extreme democracy.... Doubtless in ancient times and among some nations the artisan class were slaves or foreigners, and therefore the majority of them are so now. The best form of State will not admit them to citizenship...."

He admits that democracy may be considered as a form of government ("... if democracy be a real form of government...."), and he admits too that "... multitudes, of which each individual is but an ordinary person, when they meet together, may very likely be better than the few good, if regarded not individually but collectively.... Hence the many are better judges than a single man of music and poetry; for some understand one part, and some another, and among them they understand the whole. [Observe that he is still speaking of a democracy in which slaves and artisans are not citizens.] Doubtless too democracy is the most tolerable of perverted governments, and Plato has already made these distinctions, but his point of view is not the same as mine. For he lays down the principle that of all good constitutions democracy is the worst, but the best of bad ones." But still Aristotle cannot help thinking that democracy is a sociological mistake "... It must be admitted that we cannot raise to the rank of citizens all those, even the most useful, who are necessary to the existence of the State."

Democracy has this drawback that it cannot constitutionally retain within itself and encourage eminent men. In a democracy "if there be some one person or more than one, although not enough to make up the whole complement of a State, whose virtue is so pre-eminent that the virtues or the capacity of all the rest admit of no comparison with his or theirs, he or they can be no longer regarded as part of a State; for justice will not be done to the superior, if he is reckoned only as the equal of those who are so far inferior to him in virtue and in political capacity. Such an one may truly be deemed a God among men. Hence we see that legislation is necessarily concerned only with those who are equal in birth and in power; and that for men of pre-eminent virtue there is no law—they are themselves a law.

Anyone would be ridiculous who attempted to make laws for them: they would probably retort what, in the fable of Antisthenes, the lions said to the hares—'where are your claws?'—when in the council of the beasts the latter began haranguing and claiming equality for all. And for this reason democratic States have instituted ostracism; equality is above all things their aim, and therefore they ostracise and banish from the city for a time those who seem to predominate too much through their wealth, or the number of their friends, or through any other political influence. Mythology tells us that the Argonauts left Heracles behind for a similar reason; the ship Argo would not take him because she feared that he would have been too much for the rest of the crew."

Thrasybulus, the tyrant of Miletus, asked Periander, the tyrant of Corinth, one of the seven sages of Greece, for advice on the art of government. Periander made no reply but proceeded to bring a field of corn to a level by cutting off the tallest ears. "This is a policy not only expedient for tyrants or in practice confined to them, but equally necessary in oligarchies and democracies. Ostracism is a measure of the same kind, which acts by disabling and banishing the most prominent citizens."

This is what we may call a constitutional necessity for the democracy.

To be quite honest, it is not always obliged to cut off the ears of corn. It has a simpler method. It can systematically prevent any man who betrays any superiority whatsoever, either of birth, fortune, virtue or talent, from obtaining any authority or social responsibility. It can "send to Coventry." I have often pointed out that under the first democracy Louis XVI was guillotined for having wished to leave the country, while under the third democracy his great-nephews were exiled for wishing to remain in it. Ostracism is, in these instances, still feeling its way, and its action is contradictory because it has not made up its mind. This will continue till it has been reduced to a science, when it will contrive to level, by one method or another, every individual eminence, great and small, that dares to vary by the merest fraction from the regulation standards. This is ostracism, and ostracism, so to speak, is a physiological organ of democracy. Democracy by using it mutilates the nation, without it democracy would mutilate itself.

Aristotle often tries to solve the problem of the eminent man. "Good men," he says, "differ from any individual of the many, as the beautiful are said to differ from those who are not beautiful, and works of art from realities, because in them the scattered elements are combined.... Whether this principle can apply to every democracy and to all bodies of men is not clear.... But there may be bodies of men about whom our statement is nevertheless true. And if so, the difficulty which has been already raised—viz., what power should be assigned to the mass of freemen and citizens—is solved. There is still a danger in allowing them to share the great offices of State, for their folly will lead them into error and their dishonesty into crime. But there is a danger also in not letting them share, for a State in which many poor men are excluded from office will necessarily be full of enemies. The only way of escape is to assign to them some deliberative and judicial functions.... But each individual left to himself, forms an imperfect judgment."

It is not only the eminent man that is the thorn in the flesh of democracies, but every form of superiority, whether individual or collective, which exists outside the State and the Government.

If we recollect that Aristotle coupled extreme democracy with tyranny, it will be interesting to recall his summary of the "ancient prescriptions for the preservation of a tyranny...."

"The tyrant should lop off those who are too high; he must put to death men of spirit: he must not allow common meals, clubs, education and the like; he must be upon his guard against anything which is likely to inspire either courage or confidence among his subjects; he must prohibit literary assemblies or other meetings for discussion, and he must take every means to prevent people from knowing one another (for acquaintance begets mutual confidence)." Aristotle's conclusions are subjectively aristocratic: "In the perfect State there would be great doubts about the use of ostracism, not when applied to excess in strength, wealth, popularity or the like, but when used against some one who is pre-eminent in virtue. What is to be done with him? Mankind will not say that such an one is to be expelled and exiled; on the other hand he ought not to be a subject, that would be as if men should claim to rule over Zeus on the principle of rotation of office. The only alternative is that all should joyfully obey such a rule, according to what seems to be the order of nature, and that men like him should be kings in their State for life." But when he speaks objectively, Aristotle comes to another conclusion, which we shall have occasion to mention later on.

Among moderns, Rousseau declared that he was not a democrat, and he was right, because by democracy he meant the Athenian system of direct government, of which he did not for an instant approve. In the "Social Contract" he has drawn up a most detailed scheme, which, in spite of some contradictions and obscure passages, is an exact description of democracy as we understand the word; but still we cannot tell if he is actually a democrat, because we do not know what he means by "citizens," whether he means everybody or only one class, though that a numerous one. Rousseau has written more fully than anyone else, not so much of the influence of democracy on morals, as of the *coincidence* between democracy and good morals. Equality, frugality and simplicity can all be found, according to Rousseau, in States where there is neither royalty nor aristocracy nor plutocracy. As I understand it, his meaning is that the same virtue which makes certain nations love equality, frugality and simplicity is also productive of a form of government which excludes aristocracy, plutocracy and royalty. If you have simplicity, frugality and equality, you will probably live in a republic that is democratic or virtually democratic. This is, I think, the clearest and most impartial summary that we can make of Rousseau's doctrine, which, though set forth in rigid formulæ, is still extremely vague.

In this he is a far more faithful follower of Montesquieu than he will allow. All that I have quoted is to be found literally in Montesquieu's chapters on democracy. Even his famous saying, "the ruling principle of democracy is virtue," means, when he uses it in one sense, no more than that it is the synthesis of these three perfections, equality, simplicity and frugality. For Montesquieu sometimes uses "virtue" in a narrow, and sometimes in a broad sense, sometimes in the sense of political and civic virtue or patriotism, sometimes in the sense of virtue properly speaking (simplicity, frugality, thrift, equality). In this latter case he and Rousseau are absolutely agreed.

Montesquieu only considers democracy in decadence, as his custom is in respect of other forms of government, and though he does not actually cite Plato, he really gives the substance of what we have already quoted. "When the people wishes to do the work of the magistrates, the dignity of the office disappears and when the deliberations of the Senate carry no weight, neither senators nor old men are treated with respect. When old men do not receive respect, fathers cannot expect it from their children, husbands from their wives, nor masters from their men. At length everyone will learn to rejoice in this untrammelled liberty, and will grow as weary of commanding as of obeying. Women, children and slaves will submit to no authority. There will be an end of morals, no more love of order, no more virtue."

Now as to this transition, this passage from the public morals of a democracy to the private, domestic, personal morals which exist under that form of government, have you observed what is the common root of our failings both public and private? The common root of both is misunderstanding, forgetfulness and contempt of competence. If pupils despise their masters, young men despise old men, if wives do not respect their husbands and the unenfranchised do not respect the citizens, if the condemned do not stand in awe of their judges, nor sons in awe of their parents, the principle of efficiency has vanished. Pupils no longer admit the scientific superiority of their teachers, young men have no regard for the experience of the old, women will not recognise the supremacy of their husbands in practical matters, the unenfranchised have no sense of the superiority of the citizens from the point of view of national tradition, the condemned do not feel the moral supremacy of their judges, and sons do not realise the scientific, practical, civic and moral superiority of their fathers.

Indeed, why should they? How could we expect these feelings to be of anything but the most transient description since the State itself is organised on a basis of contempt for competence, or of what is even worse, a reverence for incompetence, and an insatiable craving for the guidance and government of the incompetent?

Thus public morals have a great influence on private morals; and gradually into family and social life there comes that laxity in the daily relations of the citizens which Plato has wittily termed, "equality between things that are equal and those that are not."

The first innovation which democracy brings into family life is the equality of the sexes, and this is followed by woman's disrespect for man. This idea, be it admitted, is substantially correct, it only ceases to be true when it is viewed relatively to the varying competences of the two sexes. Woman is man's equal in cerebral capacity, and in civilised societies, where intellect is the only thing that matters, the woman is the equal of the man. She should be admitted to the same employments as men in society, and under the same conditions of capacity and education, but in family life the same rules should apply as in every other enterprise; (1) division of labour according to the competence of each; (2) recognition of a leader according to the competence of each. This is the law which women are constantly led to misunderstand in a democracy. They will not admit the principle of the division of labour either in the world at large or in the domestic circle. They try to encroach upon men's work, which perhaps they might do very successfully, if they were obliged to do it and had nothing else at all to do; but which they really spoil by undertaking when they have other obvious duties to perform. They will not admit that men should be at the head of affairs; they aspire to be not only partners but managing directors. This implies a contemptuous rejection of that form of social competence which comes from the acceptance of convention or contract. No doubt a woman would be just as good a tax-collector as her husband, but since they have entered into partnership, the one to administer the collection of taxes, the other to look after the house, it is just as bad for the one whose business it is to keep house to begin collecting taxes, as it is for the tax-collector to interfere with the housekeeping. It is necessary to respect the efficiency that arises out of the observance of convention and contract. This, with practice and experience, will quickly become a very real and a very valuable efficiency, but if thwarted from outside will lead to friction, insecurity and disorganisation.

It is particularly by their contempt, which they are at no pains to disguise, for the competence that comes from contract and later from habit, by their refusal to recognise the position of the head of the family, that women every day and in every minute particular are training their children to despise their father. Democracy seems bent on bringing up its children to despise their parents. No other construction can be put upon the facts, however good and innocent the motives. Just sum up the facts. In the first place democracy denies that the living can be guided by the dead; it is one of its fundamental axioms that no generation should be tied and bound by its predecessor. What inference can children be expected to draw from this except that they owe no obedience to their father and mother?

Children have naturally only too great a tendency to look down on their parents. They are proud of their physical superiority; they know that their star is rising while that of their parents is setting. They are imbued with the universal prejudice of modern humanity that *progress is constant* and that therefore whatever is of yesterday is *ex hypothesi* inferior to that which is of to-day. They are driven also, as I am constrained to believe, by a sort of Nemesis inspired by fear lest human science and power should hurry forward too fast if the children were content to pick up the burden of life where their parents left it, and simply followed their fathers and did not insist on effacing all that their fathers had done and beginning again—with the result that the edifice never rises far above its foundations, and that children for this and other reasons have a natural inclination to treat their parents as Cassandras. Then, as it were to clench the argument, democracy is ready with its teaching that each generation is independent of the other, and that the dead have no lesson to impart to the living.

In the second place, democracy, applying the principle still further and proclaiming the doctrine that the State is master of all, withdraws the child from the family, as often and as completely as it can. "Democracy," said Socrates, in one of his humorous dialogues, "is a mountebank, a kidnapper of children. It snatches the child from its family while he is playing, takes him far away, allows him no more to see his family, teaches him many strange languages, drills him till his joints are supple, paints his face and dresses him in ridiculous clothes, and imparts to him all the mysteries of the acrobat's trade until he is sufficiently dexterous to appear in public and amuse the company by his tricks."

At all events democracy is determined to take the child away from his family, to give him the education which it has chosen and not that which the parents have chosen, and to teach him that he must not believe what his parents teach him. It denies the competence of parents to rear their children and puts forward its own competence, asserting that it is only its own that has any value.

This is one of the principal causes of the divisions between fathers and children in a democracy.

You may retort that democracy does not always succeed in its efforts to separate children from their parents, because there is nothing to prevent the children extending the contempt, which for such excellent reasons they have been taught to entertain for their parents, to their State-appointed teachers.

This is a most pertinent observation, for the general maxims of democracy are just as likely to make pupils despise their masters as to make sons despise their fathers. The master, too, represents in the eyes of his pupil that past which has no connection with the present and which by the law of progress is very inferior to the present. This is true; but the end of all is that between the school which counteracts the influence of the parents and the home which counteracts the influence of the school, the child becomes a personage who is never educated at all. He is in like case with a child who in the family itself receives lessons, and what is more important, example, from a mother who is religious and from a father who is an atheist. He is not educated, he has had no sort of education. The only real education, that is to say, the only transmission to the children of the ideas of their parents consists of an education at home which is reinforced by the instruction of masters chosen by the parents in accordance with their own views. This is precisely the form of education to which democracy refuses to be reconciled.

There is a still more cogent reason why old men are neither respected nor honoured in a democracy. Here is yet another efficiency formally denied and formally set aside. An interesting treatise might be written on the rise and fall of old men. Civilization has not been kind to them. In primitive times, as among savage races to-day, old men were kings. Gerontocracy, that is, government by the aged, is the most ancient form of government. It is easy to understand why this should be. In primitive ages, all knowledge was experience and the old men possessed all the historical, social and political experience of the State. They were held in great honour and listened to with the profoundest respect and veneration, in fact with an almost superstitious reverence. Nietzsche was thinking of those days when he said: "Respect for the aged is the symbol of aristocracy," and when he added: "Respect for the aged is respect for tradition," he was thinking of the reason for this assumption. That the dead should rule the living was accepted instinctively, and it was their nearness to death which evoked honour for the aged.

At a later stage the old man shared in the civil government with monarchy, aristocracy or oligarchy, and retained an almost complete control of judicial affairs. His moral and technical efficiency were still appreciated. His moral efficiency to his contemporaries consisted in the fact that his passions were deadened and his judgment as disinterested as was humanly possible. Even his obstinacy is rather an advantage than otherwise. He is not liable to whims and fancies and sudden gusts of temper or to external influence. His technical efficiency is considerable, because he has seen and remembered much and his mind has unconsciously drawn up a reference book of cases. As history repeats itself with very slight alterations, every fresh case which arises is already well known to him; it does not take him by surprise and he has a solution at hand which only requires very slight modification.

All this, however, is very ancient history. That which undermined the authority of old men was the book. Books contain all science, equity, jurisprudence and history better, it must be confessed, than the memories of old men. One fine day the young men said: "The old men were our books; now that we have books we have no further need for old men."

This was a mistake; the knowledge which is accumulated in books can never be anything but the handmaiden of living science, the science which is being constantly remodelled and corrected by living thought. A book is a wise man paralysed; the wise man is a book which still thinks and writes.

These ideas did not hold; the book superseded the old man, and the old man no longer was a library to the nation.

Later still, for various reasons, the old men drifted from a position of respect to one of ridicule. Undoubtedly they lend themselves to this; they are obstinate, foolish, prosy, boring, crotchety and unpleasant to look upon. Comic writers poked fun at these failings which are only too self-evident and showered ridicule upon them. Then as the majority of audiences is composed of young men, first of all because there are more young men than old, and secondly because old men do not often go to the theatre, authors of comic plays were certain of raising a laugh by turning old men into ridicule, or rather by exposing only their ridiculous characteristics.

At Athens and at Rome and probably elsewhere, the old man was one of the principal grotesque characters. These things, as Rousseau pointed out, have a great effect upon morals. Once the old man became a recognised traditional stage-butt, his social authority had come to an end. In the *de Senectute* it is obvious that Cicero is running counter to the stream in seeking to restore to favour a character about whom the public is indifferent and for whom all he can do is to plead extenuating circumstances.

It is a remarkable fact that even in mediæval epics, Charlemagne himself, the emperor of the flowing beard, often plays a comic part. The epic is invaded by the atmosphere of the fable.

During the Renaissance, the seventeenth and eighteenth centuries, the old man is generally, though not invariably, held up to ridicule.

Molière takes his lead from Aristophanes and Plautus rather than from Terence and is the scourge of old age as well as "the scourge of the ridiculous"; he pursues the old as a hound his prey and never leaves them in peace either in his poetry or his prose.

We must do this much justice to Rousseau that both he and his child, the Revolution, tried to restore the old man to his former glory; he makes honourable mention of him in his writings, and she gives him important posts in public ceremonies and national fêtes. Therein were received the ancient memories of Lacedæmon and of early Rome, combined with a form of reaction against the days of Louis XIV and Louis XV.

But with the triumph of democracy the old man was finally banished to the limbo of discredited things. Montesquieu's advice was quite forgotten (see the context Laws, v, 8). He said that *in a democracy* "nothing kept the standard of morals so high as that young men should venerate the old. Both profit by it, the young because they respect the old, and the old because they are confirmed in their respect for themselves" (for the respect of the young is an assistance to the self-respect of the aged).

Democracy has forgotten this advice, because it no longer believes in tradition and believes too much in progress. Old men are the natural upholders of tradition, and we must confess that an enthusiastic faith in the value of what we call progress is not commonly their failing. For this very reason their influence would be a most wholesome corrective to the system, or rather to the attitude of mind, which despises the past and sees in every change a step in the path of progress. But democracy will not allow that it needs a corrective, and the old man, to it, is only an enemy. The old man upholds tradition and has no enthusiasm for progress, but beyond this he appeals for respect, first for himself, then for religion, for glory, for his country and for the history of his nation. Democracy is indifferent to the sentiment of respect, or rather it lives in constant fear that the sentiment may be applied elsewhere.

Then what does democracy want for itself?

Not respect, but adoration, passion, devotion. We all like to see our own sentiments as to ourselves repeated in the minds of others. The crowd never respects, it loves, it yields to passion, enthusiasm, fanaticism. It never respects even that which it loves.

It is quite natural that the masses should not care for old men. The masses are young. How aptly does Horace's description of the young man apply to the people!

Imberbis juvenis, tandem custode remoto Gaudet equis, canibusque et aprici gramine campi;
Cereus in vitium flecti, monitoribus asper, Utilium tardus provisor, prodigus æris, Sublimis, cupidusque et amata relinquere pernix.

"Once free from the control of his tutors, the young man thinks of nothing but horses, dogs and the Campus Martius, impressionable as wax to every temptation, impatient of correction, unthrifty, extravagant, presumptuous and light of love."

At all events respect has no meaning for the crowd, and when it rules, we cannot from its example learn the lessons of respect. Democracy has no love for the old; and it is interesting to note that the word gerontocracy to which the ancients attached the most honourable meaning is now only a term of ridicule, and is applied only to a government which, because it is in the hands of old men, is therefore grotesque.

This disappearance of respect, noted as we have seen by Plato, Aristotle and Montesquieu as a morbid system, is, regard it how we will, a fact of the gravest import. Kant has asked the question, what must we obey? What criterion is there to tell us what to obey? What is there within us which commands respect, which does not ask for love or fear, but for respect alone? He has given us the answer. The feeling of respect is the only thing that we can trust, and that will never fail us.

In society the only feelings we obey are those which win our respect, and the men to whom we listen, and whom we honour, are those who inspire respect. This is the only criterion which enables us to gauge correctly the men and things to whom we owe, if not absolute obedience, at least attention and deference. Old men are the nation's conscience, and it is a conscience at times severe, morose, tiresome, obstinate, over-scrupulous, dictatorial, and it repeats for ever the same old saws; in other words a conscience; but conscience it is.

The comparison might be carried further with results that would be advantageous as well as curious. We degrade and finally vitiate our conscience if we do not respect its behests. Conscience then itself becomes small and timid and humble, shamefaced, and at length a mere whisper. Absolutely silent it can never be made.

It becomes sophisticated, it begins to employ the language of passion, not of the vilest passions of our nature, but still the voice of passion; it ceases to use the categoric imperative and tries to be persuasive. It no longer raises the finger of command, but it seeks to cajole with caressing hand.

Then it falls still lower, it affects indifference and scepticism and it puts on the air of the trifler in order to insinuate a word of wisdom into the seductive talk that is heard around it, and it holds language somewhat as follows: "Probably everything has its good points and there is something to be said for both vice and virtue, crime and honesty, sin and innocence, rudeness and politeness, licence and purity. These are all simply different forms of an activity which cannot be wholly wrong in any of its manifestations; and it is precisely because every one of these has its value that there may be nothing to lose in being honest, nay, perhaps something to gain."

Nevertheless, a nation that does not respect its old men changes their nature and despoils them of their beauty and integrity. How true is Montesquieu's saying that the respect paid them by the young helps old men to respect themselves! Old men who are not respected take no interest in their natural duties; they cease to advise, or else they only venture to advise indirectly, as though they were apologising for their wisdom, or they affect a laxity of morals to enable them to insinuate a surreptitious dose of worldly wisdom;—and worst of all in view of the insignificant part assigned to them in society, old men will nowadays decline to be old.

CHAPTER IX.
MANNERS.

If the worship of incompetence reverberates with a jarring note through our domestic morals, it has an effect hardly less harmful on the social relations of men in the wider theatre of public life. We often ask why politeness is out of date, and everyone replies with a smile: "This is democratic." So it is, but why should it be? Montesquieu remarks that "to cast off the conventions of civility is to seek a method for putting our faults at their ease." He adds the rather subtle distinction that "politeness flatters the vices of others, and civility prevents us from displaying our own. It is a barrier raised by men to prevent them from corrupting each other." That which flatters vice can hardly be called politeness, but is rather adulation. Civility and politeness are only slightly different in degree; civility is cold and very respectful, politeness has a suggestion of flattery. It graciously draws into evidence the good qualities of our neighbour, not his failings, much less his vices.

There is no doubt that civility and politeness are a delicate means of showing respect to our fellow-men, and of communicating a wish to be respected in turn. These things then are barriers, but barriers from which we derive support, which separate and strengthen us, but which, though holding us apart, do not keep us estranged from our neighbours.

It is also very true that if we release ourselves from these rules, whether they are civility or politeness, we set our faults at liberty. The basis of civility and politeness is respect for others and respect for ourselves. As Abbé Barthélemy has very justly remarked: "In the first class of citizens is to be found a spirit of decorum which makes it evident that men respect themselves, and a spirit of politeness which makes it evident that they also respect others." This is what Pascal meant by saying that respect is our own inconvenience, and he explains it thus, that to stand when our neighbour is seated, to remove our hat when he is covered, though trifling acts of courtesy, are tokens of the efforts we would willingly make on his behalf if an opportunity of being really serviceable to him presented itself.

Politeness is a mark of respect and a promise of devotion.

All this is anti-democratic, because democracy does not recognise any superiority, and therefore has no sympathy with respect and personal devotion. Respect to others involves a recognition from us that we are of less importance than they, and politeness to an equal requires from us a courteous affectation that we consider him as our superior. This is entirely contrary to the democratic ideal, which asserts that there is no superiority anywhere. As for pretending to treat your equal as though he were your superior, that involves a double hypocrisy, because it requires a reciprocal hypocrisy on the part of your neighbour. You praise his wit, only in order that he may return the compliment.

Without, however, insisting on this point, democracy will argue that politeness is to be deprecated, because it not only recognises but actually creates superiority. It treats an equal as a superior, as though there were not enough discrepancies already without inventing any more. It seems to imply that if inequality did not exist, it would be necessary to invent it. It is tantamount to proclaiming that there cannot be too much aristocracy. That is an opinion which democracy cannot endure.

Considered as a promise of future devotion, politeness is equally anti-democratic. The citizen owes no devotion to any person, he owes it only to the community. It is no small matter to style yourself "your most humble servant"; it means that you single out one man from among many others and promise to serve him; it means that you acknowledge in him some natural or social superiority, and according to democracy there are no superiorities, social or natural, and if there were such a thing as natural superiority, nature has no business to allow it. This is tantamount to proclaiming a form of vassalage—a thing which is not to be tolerated.

As to the absence of politeness considered as "a means of giving free play to one's feelings," we recognise that in one sense this also is essentially democratic. The democrat is not proud of or pleased with his faults; not at all; only *ex hypothesi* he does not believe in their existence. A failing is an inferiority of one man in relation to another; the word itself implies it; it means that something is lacking, that one man has a thing which another has not. But all men are equal, therefore, argues the democrat, I have no failing; therefore I need not try to conceal and control my alleged failings, as they are at worst merely mannerisms, and are possibly virtues.

The democrat, in fact, like young men, like most women, and like all human beings who have begun to think but do not think very profoundly, knows his failings and assumes that they are virtues. This is very natural, for our faults are the most conspicuous parts of our character, and when we are still at the self-satisfied stage it is our faults that we cherish and admire. Consequently, politeness, in that it consists in concealing our faults, is intolerable to a man who is impatient to display qualities that to him appear commendable and worthy. The usual reason why we do not correct our faults is that we mistake them for qualities, and think that any practice which requires their concealment must be quite absurdly tyrannical.

The democrat is therefore profoundly convinced of two things; first, that all men are equal and that there is no such thing as inferiority or failing, and secondly, that what men call faults are really natural characteristics of great interest. He believes that faults are popular prejudices invented by intriguers, priests, nobles and rulers, for their own base purposes to inspire the poor with humility. He looks upon this sense of inferiority as a curb on the people's power, all the more potent that it works from within and has a paralysing effect on its energy. He is persuaded that, from this point of view, politeness is an aristocratic instrument of tyranny.

This explains why, when the wave of democracy swept over France, it brought with it a perfect frenzy of rudeness, all the more curious in a nation remarkable for courtesy. It was an affirmation that, appearances notwithstanding, neither superiorities nor excellences of human character had any real existence.

Rudeness is democratic.

CHAPTER X.
PROFESSIONAL CUSTOMS.

The contempt for efficiency is carried far even in the liberal professions and in professional customs. We all know the story, perhaps a mythical one, of the judge who said to an earnest young barrister who was conscientiously elaborating a question of law: "Now, Mr. So and So, we are not here to discuss questions of law but to settle this business." He did not say this by way of jest; he wished to say: "The courts no longer deliver judgment on the merits of a case according to law, but according to equity and common sense. The intricacies of the law are left to professors, so please when conducting a case do not behave like a professor of law." This theory, which even in this mild form would have horrified the ancients, is very prevalent nowadays in legal circles. It has crept in as an infiltration, as one might call it, from the democratic system.

A magistrate, nowadays, whatever remnant of the ancient feeling of caste he may have retained, certainly does not consider himself bound by the letter of the law, or by jurisprudence, the written tradition; when he is anything more than a subordinate with no other idea of duty than subservience to the Government, he is a democratic magistrate, a Heliast of Athens; he delivers judgment according to the dictates of his individual conscience; he does not consider himself as a member of a learned body, bound to apply the decisions of that body, but as an independent exponent of the truth.

An eccentric, but in truth very significant, example of the new attitude of mind is to be found in the judge, who formally attributed to himself the right to make law and who in his judgments made references, not to existing laws, but to such vague generalities as appealed to him, or to doctrines which he prophesied would *later on* be embodied in the law. His Code was the Code of the future.

The mere existence of such a man is of no particular importance, but the fact that many people, even those partially enlightened, took him seriously, that he was popular, and that a considerable faction thought him a good judge, is most significant.

There is another much commoner sign of the times. The worst form of incompetence is perhaps that which allows a man to be competent without realising it, and, in criminal cases at least, this seems to be the normal attitude of the majority of our magistrates.

We should read on this point a very curious pamphlet called *Le Pli Professionnel* (1909), by Marcel Lestranger, a provincial magistrate. It is very pertinent to our subject. It shows plainly that the magistracy nowadays, both the qualified stipendiaries and the bench of magistrates, has lost all confidence in itself and is terrified of public opinion as represented by newspapers, associations, political clubs and the man in the street; the magistrate knows too, or thinks he knows, that promotion depends, not on a reputation for severity as it used to do, but on a reputation for indulgence.

He is confronted in the execution of his duty by forces which are always in coalition against him; the public, almost always favourable to the accused, the press, both local and Parisian, the so-called science of judicial medicine, which is almost always disposed to consider the accused as persons not responsible for their actions. He lives, too, in constant terror of being mixed up in a miscarriage of justice, for miscarriage of justice is now a sort of craze, and with a considerable section of the public every conviction is a miscarriage of justice. And so the magistrate of first instance never dares to sum up severely, and the stipendiary never dares press his interrogations with firmness.

There are exceptions of course; but these exceptions, by the astonishment which they excite, and by the reaction to which they give rise, show sufficiently, indeed conclusively, that they are abnormal, outside the new order of things, outside the new habits of the people.

More often than not the subordinate magistrate, whose business it is to commit the prisoner for trial, acts with timidity and reserve, apologetically attenuating the crime; he leaves loopholes of escape, appeals in audible asides for indulgence, dwells on the uncertainty of evidence. He demands indeed the prisoner's head but lives in terror lest he obtain it.

The fact is what both he and the stipendiary desire is that the affair should be settled by an acquittal, for an affair settled by an acquittal is an affair buried. Stone-dead has no fellow; it is consigned to oblivion. It can never be made the sort of affair which someone is sure to declare is a miscarriage of justice, or which someone, animated by private and political spite or merely for the sake of a jest, can make into a ghost to haunt for ten or even fifteen years the unfortunate magistrate who had to deal with it.

M. Lestranger tells a story which, from all the information I can glean and from what I can remember hearing at the time, is absolutely true and a perfect illustration of thousands of similar cases.

A poacher, aged nineteen, first outraged and then strangled in the woods a peasant woman, the mother of a family. On this occasion there could be no question of a miscarriage of justice or even of any suggestion of such a thing, because the prisoner pleaded guilty. That is a great point. In France every conviction that is not based upon the prisoner's confession is a miscarriage of justice; but when the prisoner pleads guilty there can be no incriminations of this sort, although there might be, for false confessions are not unknown, but nothing of the sort is ever put forward, and the case seemed to be quite straightforward.

But the magistrates were terrified that the prisoner would be condemned to death. The crime was horrible, particularly in the eyes of a village jury, whose wives and daughters were often obliged to work some distance from the village. Moreover, there was a tiresome man, the widower of the victim, thirsting for vengeance, who sang the praises of his wife and brought his weeping son into court while he gave his evidence. The president and the public prosecutor were in despair.

"I have done all I can," said the president to the public prosecutor. "I have made the most of his youth. I have repeated 'only nineteen years of age.' I have indeed done all I can."

"I have done all I can," said the public prosecutor to the president. "I have not said a word about the punishment. I merely accused. I could not plead for the defence. I have done my best."

At the close of the hearing the chief constable was very reassuring to these gentlemen. "He is under twenty and he looked so respectable at the enquiry. It is quite impossible that he should be condemned to death in this quiet village. You will see, he will not be sentenced to capital punishment."

He was not. The jury brought in a verdict of guilty with extenuating circumstances. The magistrates recovered their tranquillity.

M. Lestranger's facts are supported by figures. Those who commit crimes which excite pity, such as infanticide and abortion, are less and less likely to be prosecuted, and if they are, they are frequently let off, however flagrant the offence. The average number of acquittals during the last twelve years is twenty-six per cent. A magistrate nowadays is a St. Francis of Assize.

Either the magistrate does not believe in his own efficiency, or he sacrifices it to his peace of mind, and he cares more for his own peace of mind than for the public safety. The magistracy will soon be no more than a *façade*, still imposing but not at all alarming.

There is already a very serious symptom of how little confidence the crowd has in the wholesome severities of justice; the criminal caught in the act is often lynched or almost lynched, because it is well known that if he is not punished immediately, he is very likely to escape punishment altogether.

—Yet this same crowd, in the form of a jury, is often, almost always, very indulgent.— True, and that is because between the crime and the assizes there is often an interval of six months. At the date of the crime it is the misfortune of the victim that excites the crowd, at the date of the assize it is the misfortune of the accused. Be this as it may, the practice of lynching amounts to a formal accusation that both magistrates and juries are over indulgent.

The clergy even, who are more tenacious of tradition than any other order in the State, are gradually becoming democratic to this extent, that though by profession teachers of dogmas and mysteries, they now teach only morality. In this way they try to get into closer touch with the poor, and so have a greater hold upon them. Evidently they are not altogether to blame. Only, when they cease to teach dogma and interpret mysteries, they cease to be a learned body or to have the prestige of a learned body. On the other hand they sink to the level of any other philosophy, which teaches and explains morality, and illustrates it by sacred examples just as well as any priesthood. The result is that the people say to themselves "What need have we of priests? Moral philosophers are good enough for us."

This Americanism is not very dangerous, in fact it does not matter, in America, where there are very few lay moral philosophers; but it is a very great danger in France, Italy and Belgium where their name is legion.

In every profession, to sum it all up, the root of the evil is this, that we believe that mere dexterity and cunning are incomparably superior to knowledge and that cleverness is infinitely more valuable than sound learning. Those who follow professions believe this, and the lay public that employs the professions is not dismayed by this attitude of the professional class; and so things tend to that equality of charlatanry to which democracy instinctively tends. Democracy does not respect efficiency, but it soon will have no opportunity to respect it; for efficiency is being destroyed and before long will have disappeared altogether. There will soon be no difference between the judge and the suitor, between the layman and the priest, the sick man and the physician. The contempt which is felt for efficiency destroys it little by little, and efficiency, accepting the situation, outruns the contempt that is felt for it. The end will be that we shall all be only too much of one opinion.

CHAPTER XI.
ATTEMPTED REMEDIES.

We have sought very conscientiously, and democrats themselves have sought very conscientiously, to find remedies for this constitutional disease of democracy. We have preserved certain bodies, relatively aristocratic, as refuges, we would fain believe, of efficiency. We have preserved for instance a Senate, elected by universal suffrage, not directly, but in the second degree. We have preserved also a Parliament (a

Senate and a Chamber of Deputies), a floating aristocracy which is continually being renewed. This is, however, in a sense an aristocracy inasmuch as it stands between us and a direct and immediate government of the people by the people.

These remedies are by no means to be despised, but we recognise that they are very feeble, for the reason that democracy always eludes them. By the care it takes to exclude efficiency, it has made the Chamber of Deputies (with some few exceptions) a body resembling itself with absolute fidelity both in respect of the superficial character of its knowledge and the violence of its prejudices; with the result in my opinion that the crowd might just as well govern directly and, without the intervention of representatives, by means of the plebiscite.

The same thing applies to the Senate, though perhaps in a more direct fashion. The Senate is chosen by the delegates of universal suffrage. These delegates, however, are not chosen by a general universal suffrage where each department would choose four or five hundred delegates, but by the town councillors of each commune or parish. In these communes, especially in the rural communes, the municipal councillors who are by far the most numerous and, with regard to elections, the most influential, are more or less completely dependent on the *préfets*. The result is that the Senate is, practically, chosen by the *préfets*, that is, by the Government, as used to be the case under the First and Second Empire. The maker of the constitution made this arrangement for the benefit of his own party, for he upheld authority; and he wanted the Central Government to control the elections of the Senate. It has not turned out as he intended. *Vos non vobis*, others have profited by his device, as the following considerations will show.

It is well known that in France a deputy belonging to the opposition, though sure of his constituents, and certain to be re-elected indefinitely, who for private reasons wishes to be a senator, is obliged to be civil to the Government in power, to abate his opposition, and to make himself pleasant, if he wishes to avoid failure in his new ambition. It is very inconvenient to have a strong and active opposition in the Senate.

It comes back again to this, that we have a Senate not far removed from one elected by universal suffrage.

Universal suffrage elects the Chamber of Deputies, the Chamber elects the Government, and the Government elects the Senate. The Senate is therefore an extremely feeble anti-democratic remedy, and if it were intended as a check on democracy, it has not been a striking success.

If we really wish to have an upper chamber as competent as possible, independent of the central authority, and relatively independent of universal suffrage, we must establish a chamber elected by the great constituent bodies of the nation, and also in my opinion, by universal suffrage, but with modifications somewhat as follows. The whole nation, divided for practical purposes into five or six large districts, should elect five or six thousand delegates who in turn should elect three hundred senators. There would then be no pressure from Government nor any manufacture by the crowd of a representation fashioned in its own image, and we should have a really select body composed of as much competence as could be got in the country.

It is, however, exactly the opposite of this that is done, and the French Senate is an extremely feeble, anti-democratic remedy.

It represents the rural democracy, arbitrarily guided and governed by the democratic Government.

Another remedy which has been given an equally conscientious trial is the system of competitive examination, which is supposed to be a guarantee for the ability of those who seek admission into government service. The object of these examinations, which are extremely detailed and complicated, is to test the ability of the candidate in every particular, to give employment to merit and to exclude favouritism.

—You call that an anti-democratic remedy! It is as democratic as well can be!—

Nay, pardon! It would be anti-monarchical if we lived under a monarchy, anti-aristocratic if we lived under an aristocracy, and it is anti-democratic because our lot is cast in a democracy. Competition for public offices is a sort of co-optation. In fact it is co-optation pure and simple. When I suggested that the magistracy should be chosen by the magistrates, that is, the *Cour de Cassation* by the magistrates and the magistrates in turn by the *Cour de Cassation*, I was of course accused of being paradoxical, as is always the case, when one suggests something contrary to the usual custom. I was, however, only carrying a little further the principle which is already applied to officials. In a certain sense and to a large extent officials recruit their numbers by co-optation.

It is true, they do not actually choose the officials, but they eliminate the candidates whom they do not wish to have. Examination is ostracism of the inefficient. The Government, of course, has to decide who may be candidates, but its selection for employment is limited to those of whom other officials (the officials who conduct the examination) can approve. It is in fact co-optation.

The committee of examiners which admits a candidate to St. Cyr appoints an officer. The committee which admits a candidate to the *École Polytechnique* appoints an officer or an engineer. A committee also which refuses a candidate at either of these places is encroaching on the National Sovereignty, because it is forbidding the National Sovereignty to make of this young man an officer or an engineer. This is co-optation. This is a guarantee of efficiency. Here a wall is raised against incompetence, and against the jobbery under which incompetence would profit.

It is hardly necessary for me to add that this co-optation is limited to a very narrow field of operation. It is confined in fact to the threshold of a man's career. Once the candidate has been consecrated official, by a board of examining officials, he belongs, both as regards advancement, promotion and the reverse, to the central authority alone, except in certain cases. The co-optation of officials is merely a co-optation by elimination. The elimination is made once and for all, and the non-eliminated (*i.e.*, the successful candidate) steps at once into the toils of the Government, that is, into the toils of popular electioneering and party politics, when all the abuses which I have enumerated can and do arise. To be fair I had of course to point out that we had tried to invent some slight barriers against the omnipotence of incompetence, which prevent it being absolutely supreme.

Unfortunately these prophylactic measures are very badly organised, and, far from being capable of amendment, ought to be completely revolutionised.

The examination system in our country is founded on a misconception, I mean on the confusion between knowledge and competence. We search conscientiously for competence or efficiency, and we believe that we have found it when we find knowledge, but that is an error. An examination requires from a candidate that he shall know, and competition demands that he shall know more than the others, but that is almost all that examination and competition require of him. Therefrom results one of the most painful open sores of our civilisation,— preparation for examinations.

Preparation for examination is responsible for intellectual indigestion, for minds overloaded with useless information, and for a system of cramming, which at once takes the heart out of men, perhaps with good ability, just at the age when their mental activity is most keen; which, further, as the result of this surfeit, disgusts for the rest of his life and renders impotent for all intellectual effort, the unfortunate patient who has been condemned to undergo this treatment for five, eight, and sometimes ten years of his youth.

I am satisfied, if I may be allowed to speak of myself in order to support my argument by an instance well known to me, that, if I have been able to work from the age of twenty-five to that of sixty-three, it is because I have never succeeded except very moderately, and I am proud of it, in competitive examinations. Being of a curious turn of mind I have been interested in the subject set in the syllabus, but in other matters also, and the syllabus has been neglected. I sometimes passed, more often I failed, with the result that at twenty-six I was behind my contemporaries, but I was not overworked, broken down, and utterly sick of all intellectual effort. I admit that some of my contemporaries who never failed in an examination, and who passed them all with great brilliance, have worked as hard as I have up to sixty, but they are extremely few.

The curious thing is that the results, not perhaps disastrous, but obviously very unsatisfactory, of this examination system do not lead us to abandon it (that perhaps would be an extreme measure), but make us aggravate and complicate it. Legal and medical examinations are much "stiffer" than they used to be, and they require a greater physical effort, but without requiring or obtaining any greater intellectual value. In truth, one might say, examination is nothing more than a test of good health, and it is a very searching test, for it often succeeds in destroying it.

Here is an example which I know well. It is necessary, if a man desire to gain distinction as a professor of secondary education, that he should be a bachelor, a licentiate, an *agrégé* or a doctor. This is a qualification that counts, and it means ten examinations or competitions, two for the first half of the bachelor's degree, two for the second, two for the licentiate, two for *agrégé*, two for the doctor's degree. This, moreover, does not appear to be enough. Between the second part of the bachelor's degree and the licentiate's degree there is normally an interval of two years; between the licentiate and the *agrégation* two years, and between the *agrégation* and the doctor's degree there is generally three or four years. You perceive the danger! Between the *licence* and the *agrégation*, to go no further at present, the future professor has two whole years to himself. That is to say, that during the first of these two years he will work alone. He can work freely, he can study in what direction he pleases, without thinking of an examination at the end of twelve months; he has escaped for the moment from the servitude of the syllabus. The prospect makes us shudder with apprehension. It is sadly to be feared that the young man may take a rest and draw breath, or worse still he may be carried into some extraneous study by his personal aptitudes or tastes. The personality of the candidate has here an opening, a moment at which it has a possibility of asserting itself. That must be stopped at all costs.

The authorities, therefore, have put in an intermediate examination between the *licence* and the *agrégation*. The examination, it is true, is on a subject chosen by the candidate himself; so much it is only fair to admit. The subject chosen, however, must be submitted to the professors. Their advice and indeed assistance must be invited. The result, if not the object, of this examination is to prevent the candidate, during this perilous year of liberty, from developing original ideas of his own and acting on them.

One examination every year for ten years—that is the ideal of the modern professor for the future professors who are in course of being trained. Between the second part of the bachelor's degree and the licentiate, as there is there an interval of two years, they will presently perceive that there ought to be an examination at the end of the first year, and we shall have certificates of study in intermediate, secondary, higher subjects. Between the *agrégation* and the *doctorat*, there are four years, and naturally we shall want three examinations just to see how the future professor is getting on with his theses, to encumber him with assistance and to prevent him doing them alone; first examination called the *Bibliography of the Theses for the Doctorat*, second examination called the *Methodology of the Doctorat*, third examination called the *Preparation for the Sustaining of the Thesis*, and then the examination for the doctor's degree itself.

In this way the desired object is attained. Between the ages of seventeen and twenty-seven or thirty the examinee will have had to undergo sixteen examinations. He will never have worked alone. He will always have worked, for periods of twelve months, on a syllabus, for an examination, with a view of pleasing such and such professors, modelling himself on their views, their conceptions, their general ideas, their eccentricities, aided by them, influenced by them, never knowing, and feeling he ought not to know, not wishing to know, and running a great risk if he did know, and forming habits for his whole life so that he may never know what he thinks himself, what he imagines himself, what he seeks and would like to seek of his own motion, or what he ought himself to try to be. He will take up all this after he is thirty.

Not a vestige of personality or original thought till the moment when it is too late for it to appear, that is the maxim!

Whence comes this frenzy, this *examino mania*? When one comes to think of it, it seems to be a simple case of *Dandino-mania*. Dandin says with great determination "I mean to go and judge." The professor of a certain age means to go and examine. He no longer loves to profess, he loves to be always examining. This is very natural. Professing, he is judged; examining, he judges. The one is always much pleasanter than the other. For a professor, to sweat in harness, to feel oneself being examined, that is, criticised, discussed, held up to judgment, and chaffed by an audience of students and amateurs, ceases at a certain age to be altogether pleasant; on the other hand to examine, to sit on the throne with all the majesty of a judge, to have only to criticise and not to produce, to intervene only when the victim stumbles, and to let him know that he has made a slip, to hold the student for the whole year under the salutary terror of an approaching examination, to remind him that he may need help and must by no means displease his professor—all this is very agreeable and makes up for many of the worries of the teaching profession. The examination mania proceeds partly from the terror of being oneself examined, and partly from the pleasure of examining others.

All this is true, but there is more than this. The precocious development of early talent and originality is the thing which strangely terrifies these examination-maniacs. They have a horror of the man who teaches himself. They have a horror of any one who ventures to think for himself and to enquire for himself at twenty-five years of age. They want, like an old hen, to mother the young mind as long as possible. They will not let it find its own feet, till very late, and till, as the scoffer might well say, its limbs are absolutely atrophied. I do not say that they are wrong. The man who has taught himself is apt to be a vain, conceited fellow who takes pleasure in thinking for himself, and has an absolute delight in despising the thoughts of others. It is, however, no less the fact, that it is among these self-taught men that we find those vigorous spirits who venture boldly beyond the domain of human science and extend its frontier. The question then is which is best, to favour all these troublesome self-taught people in the hope of finding some good ones among them, or by crossing and worrying them to run the risk of destroying the good as well as the bad. I am myself strongly in favour of the first of these alternatives. It is better to let all go their own way, even though pretenders to originality come to grief, a thing that matters very little. Minds that are truly original will develop themselves and find room for the expansion of all their powers.

But here,—take note how the democratic spirit comes in everywhere—the question of numbers is raised. Ten times more numerous, I am told, are the pretenders to originality whom we save from themselves by discipline than the true geniuses whose wings we clip.

I reply that, in matters intellectual, questions of figures do not count. An original spirit strangled is a loss which is not compensated by the rescue of ten fools from worse excesses of folly. An original spirit left free to be himself is worth more than ten fools whose folly is partially restrained.

Nietzsche has well said: "Modern education consists in smothering the exceptional in favour of the normal. It consists in directing the mind away from the exceptional into the channel of the average." This ought not to be. I do not say that education should do the opposite of all this. Oh no, far from that. It is not the business of education to look for exceptional genius, or to help in its creation. Exceptional genius is born of itself and it has no need of such assistance. But even less is it the business of education to regard the exceptional with terror, and to take every means possible, even the most barbarous and most detailed, to prevent it as long as possible from coming to the light.

Education ought to draw all that it can out of mediocrity, and to respect originality as much as it can. It ought never to attempt to turn mediocrity into originality, nor to reduce originality to the level of mediocrity.

And how can all this be done? By an intervention that is always discreet, and sometimes by non-intervention.

At the present moment its policy is equally distant from non-intervention and from an intervention that is discreet.

It is in this way that the very institution which we have invented to safeguard efficiency contributes not a little to the triumph of its opposite. These victims of examination are competent in respect of knowledge, instruction and technical proficiency. They are incompetent in respect of intellectual value, often, though perhaps not so often as formerly, in respect of moral value.

As far as their intellectual value is concerned, they have very frequently no mental initiative. It has been cramped, hidden away, and trampled down. If it ever existed, it exists now no longer. They are all their days merely instruments. They have been taught many things, especially intellectual obedience. They continue to obey intellectually, their brain acts like well made and well lubricated machinery. "The difference between the novel and the play," said Brunetière, "is that in the play the characters act, in the novel they are acted." I do not know if this be true, but of the functionary we might say as often as not, he does not think, he is thought.

The official also is incompetent, though less and less often, in respect of moral worth. By the exercise of intellectual obedience, he has been trained to moral obedience also and he is little disposed to assert his independence. Observe how everything tends to this end. This method of co-opting officials by means of elimination, as I have said, operates only, as I have also shown, at the outset of the official's career. From this moment onwards the functionary must depend on the Government only, his whole preparation during ten years of education has been calculated to ensure his absolute dependence on his official directors. So far good, perhaps a little too good. It would have been well if the education of the functionary had left him, together with a little originality of mind, a little originality of character as well.

We have sought, very conscientiously also, and, I may even say, with an admirable enthusiasm, yet another remedy for the faults of democracy, another remedy for its incompetence. It is said: "The crowd is incompetent, so be it, it is necessary to enlighten it. Primary education, spread broadcast, is the solution of every difficulty, and provides an answer to every question."

From this argument aristocrats have derived some little amusement. "How is this?" they exclaimed, "what is the meaning of this paradox? You are democrats and that means that you attribute political excellence, 'political virtue,' as we used to say, to the crowd, that is to ignorance. Why then do you wish to enlighten the crowd, that is to destroy the very virtue which, on your own showing, is the cause of its superiority?" The democrats reply that the crowd, even as it is, is already very preferable to aristocracy, and that it will be still more so when it has received instruction. They resolve the apparent contradiction by the argument *a fortiori*.

At all events, the democrats set to work most vigorously on the education of the people. The result is that the people is much better educated than formerly, and I am one of those who regard this result as excellent; but the further result is, that the people is saturated with false ideas, and this is less comforting.

Ancient republics had their demagogues, their orators, who inflamed the evil qualities of the people, by bestowing on them high-sounding names and by flattery. The great democracy of modern times has its demagogues. These are its elementary school teachers. They come of the people, are proud to belong to it, for which of course no one can blame them, they distrust everything that is not the people, they are all the more of the people because among the people they are intellectually in the first rank while elsewhere they are of secondary importance; and what men love is not the group of which they form a part, but the group of which they are the chief. They are, therefore, profoundly democratic.

So far nothing could be better. But it is a narrow form of democratic sentiment which they hold, for they are only half-educated, or rather (for who is completely educated or even well educated?), because they have only received a rudimentary education. Rudimentary education may perhaps make us capable of having one idea, it certainly renders us incapable of having two. The man of rudimentary education is always the man of one single idea and of one fixed idea. He has few doubts. Now the wise man doubts often, the ignorant man seldom, the fool never. The man of one idea is more or less impermeable to any process of reasoning that is foreign to this idea. An Indian author has said: "You can convince the wise; you can convince, with more difficulty, the ignorant; the half-educated, never."

Now no one ever convinces the elementary schoolmaster. He is confirmed in his convictions by defending, and still more by discussing them. He is the slave of his opinion. He does not possess it always quite clearly, but it possesses him. He loves it with all his soul, as a priest his religion, because it is the truth, because it is beautiful, because it has been persecuted, and because it means the salvation of the world. He would enjoy its triumph but he yearns still more to be a martyr in its cause.

He is a convinced democrat and a sentimental democrat. His conviction forms a solid basis for his sentiment, and his sentiment kindles to a white heat his conviction. His conviction makes him turn a deaf ear to every objection, his sentiment inspires him with hatred for his adversary. For him the man who is not a democrat is wrong, and further, to him an object of hatred. In his eyes the distance between himself and the aristocrat is as the distance between truth and error, nay between good and evil, between honour and dishonour. The schoolmaster is the fanatic vassal of democracy.

Then, as he is a man of one idea, he is single-minded, narrowly logical, and logical to the utmost extreme. He goes straight forward where his argument leads. An idea which admits neither qualification nor question can go far in a very short space of time. And the schoolmaster drives all his democratic principles to their natural and logical conclusion.

He develops these principles and all that they imply by the sheer force of what he calls his "reasoning reason," and it appears to him to be not only natural but salutary to seek their realisation. Everything of which the principle is good is good itself, and no one but Montesquieu could ever believe that an institution could be ruined by the excess of the principle in which its merit consists.

The schoolmaster, therefore, deduces their logical consequences from the two great democratic principles, the sovereignty of the nation, and equality; he deduces them rigorously, and arrives at the following conclusions.

The people alone is sovereign. Therefore, though there can be individual liberty and liberty of association, there ought to be only such individual liberty and liberty of association as the people permits. Liberty cannot be and ought not to be anything more than a thing tolerated by the sovereign people. The individual may think, speak, write, and act as he pleases, but only so far as the people will allow him; for if he can do these things with absolute freedom, or even with limitations which are not imposed by the people, he becomes the sovereign power, or the power which fixed the limits of his freedom becomes the sovereign, and the sovereignty of the people disappears.

This brings us back to the simple definition that liberty is the right to do what we please within the limits of the law. And who makes the law? The people. Liberty is then the right to do everything which the people permits us to do. Nothing more; if we attempt to go beyond this, the sovereignty of the individual begins, and the sovereignty of the people disappears.

—But to have liberty to do only what the people permits, this is to be free as we were under Louis XIV.—and that is not to be free at all!

So be it. There will indeed be no liberty unless the law permit it. Surely you do not wish to be free in opposition to the law?

—The law may be tyrannical. It is tyrannical if it is unjust.—

The law has the right to be unjust. Otherwise the sovereignty of the people would be limited and this must not be.

—Fundamental and constitutional laws might be devised to limit this sovereignty of the people in order to guarantee such and such of the liberties for the individual.—

And the people would then be tied! The sovereignty of the people would be suppressed! No, the people cannot be tied. The sovereignty of the people is fundamental and must be left intact.

—Then there will be no individual liberty?—

Only such a measure as the people will tolerate.

—Then there will be no liberty of association?

Still less; for an association is in itself a limitation of the sovereignty of the nation. It has its own laws, which from a democratic point of view is an absurd and monstrous incongruity. The right of association limits the national sovereignty, just as would a free town or sanctuary of refuge. It limits the nation, and pulls it up short in face of its closed doors. It is a State within a State; where there is association, there arises at once a source of organisation other than the great organism of the popular will. It is like an animal which lives some sort of independent life within another animal larger than itself and which, living on that other animal, is still independent of it. In fact there can be only one association, the association of the nation, otherwise the sovereignty of the nation is limited, that is, destroyed. No liberty of association can then exist.

Associations of course will exist which the people will tolerate, but their right of existence[197] is always revocable and they are always liable to be dissolved and destroyed. Otherwise the national sovereignty would be held to abdicate and it can never abdicate.

—Ah! but there is one association, at least, which to some extent is sacred, and which the sovereignty of the people is bound to respect. I mean the family. The father is the head of the family, he educates his children and brings them up as he thinks best, till they come to man's estate.—

Nay, that will not pass! For here again we have a limitation of the sovereignty of the nation. The child does not belong to his father. If this were so, at the threshold of each home the sovereignty of the people would be arrested, which means that it would cease to exist anywhere. The child, like the man, belongs to the people. He belongs to it, in the sense that he must not be a member of an association which might dare to think differently from the people, or perhaps even harbour ideas in contradiction to the thought of the people. It would indeed be dangerous to leave our future citizens for twenty years outside the national thought, which is the same thing as being outside the community. Imagine five or six bees brought up apart, outside the laws, regulations, and constitution of the hive; imagine further that of these groups of bees there were several hundreds in the hive. The result would be the destruction of the hive.

It is *above all things* in the family that the sovereignty of the people ought to prevail. It ought above all things to refuse to recognise the association of the family, and to wage war against it wherever it finds it. It should leave to parents the right of embracing their children, but nothing more. The right to educate them in ideas perhaps contrary to those of their parents belongs to the people, which, here as well as elsewhere, perhaps even more than elsewhere for the interests at stake are more important, must be absolutely sovereign.

This, then, is what the schoolmaster, with a relentless logic which appears to me to be irresistible, deduces from the principle of the national sovereignty.

From the principle of equality he deduces another point. "All men are equal by nature and before the law." That is to say, if there were justice, all men ought to have been equal by nature, and further, if there is to be justice, all men ought to be equal before the law.

Very obviously, however, all men are not equal before the law, and they are not equal by nature. Very well then, we must make them so.

They are not equal before the law. They appear to be so, but they are not. The rich man, even supposing that the magistrates are perfectly and strictly honest, by reason of the fact that he can remunerate the best solicitors, advocates, and witnesses, by reason further of the fact that he intimidates by his influence all those who could appear against him, is not in every respect the equal of the poor man before the law.

Even less does this equality exist in the presence of that union of constituted social forces which we call society. In this respect the rich man will be the "influential man"; the "man well connected," the man on whom no one depends, but whom no one likes to cross or to contradict. There is, between the rich and the poor man, however equal we may pretend them to be before the law, the difference between the man who gives orders and the man who is obliged to obey. *Real* equality, in society, in presence of society and even in presence of the law, only exists where there is neither rich nor poor.

But there will always be rich and poor, as long as the institution of inheritance remains. Abolish inheritance therefore!

But, even with inheritance abolished, there will still be rich and poor. The man who can make his fortune rapidly will be a strong man relatively to the man who can not make a fortune, and, I would have you note it, even when we have abolished inheritance, the son of the strong man, during the life of his father, will be strong himself, so that even if we abolish inheritance, a privilege, namely, the privilege of birth will still exist and equality will not exist.

There is only one state of affairs under which equality is possible, that is when no one possesses and no one can acquire anything. The only social policy so devised that no one can possess and no one can acquire anything is the policy of a community of goods, that is Communism or Collectivism. Collectivism is nothing very wonderful. Collectivism is equality; and equality is collectivism, otherwise our equality will be nothing but a phantom and an hypocrisy. Every one who is a convinced and sincere *egalitarian*, and who takes the trouble to think, is forced to be a collectivist. Bonald asked very wittily: "Do you know what is a deist? It is a man who has not lived long enough to be an atheist." We in our turn ask: "Do you know what is an anti-collectivist democrat? It is a man who has not lived long enough to be a collectivist, or who, having lived long enough, has never taken the trouble to think, and to perceive what are the necessary consequences of his own principles."

But surely collectivism is a chimæra, an utopia, a thing impossible. Certainly it is impossible in the sense that in the country which adopts it the source of all initiative will be destroyed. No man will make an effort to improve his position, since it must never be improved. The whole country will become one of those stagnant pools to which one of our ministers lately referred. Everyone having become an official, everyone will realise the ideal of the official which the Goncourts have very neatly described. "The good official," they say, "is the man who combines laziness with extreme accuracy." It is a definitive definition. The country that reformed itself in this way would be conquered at the end of ten years by some neighbouring people more or less ambitious.

That admits of no question; but what does it prove? That collectivism is only impossible because it is only possible if established in every country at once. Very well, and in order to establish it in every country at once, only one thing is needful, namely, that there shall no longer be distinct and separate countries and no longer any nationalities. It surely will not answer to establish collectivism before the abolition of nationalities, since, once established, it will serve no purpose except to bring into prominent relief the vast superiority of countries which have not adopted collectivism. We must, therefore, take our problems in order and abolish nationalities before we can establish collectivism.

Now if nations organise themselves against nature (the nature that, the schoolmaster assumes, makes all men equal), if instinctively they organise themselves in a hierarchy which is aristocratic, if they have their leaders and their subordinates, their stronger and their weaker members, it is because this arrangement is necessary in a camp, and each nation feels that it is a camp. If each feels that it is a camp, it is simply because there are other nations round it, because it feels and knows that there are others round it. When there are no longer other nations, each nation will organise itself no longer against nature, but naturally, that is to say on *egalitarian* principles. Nature perhaps strictly speaking is not *egalitarian*, but it tends towards equality in the sense that it produces many more, indeed infinitely more, mediocrities than superior intelligences.

Thus equality demands the abolition of inheritance, and the equality of possessions. Equality of possessions necessitates collectivism, and collectivism requires the abolition of nationalities. We are *egalitarians*, then collectivists, and by logical consequence anti-patriots.

So argue the great majority of school teachers, with an absolute logic, in my opinion, irrefutable, with the logic which takes no account of facts, and which only takes account of its own principle and of itself. So they will all argue to-morrow, if they continue, as it is probable they will continue, to be very excellent dialecticians.

Will they go back to the premises and say, that if the sovereignty of the people and equality lead logically and imperatively to these conclusions, it is perhaps because the sovereignty of the people and equality are false ideas, and because these conclusions prove them to be false? This is a course not likely to be taken, for the sovereignty of the people and the principle of equality are something more than general ideas, they are sentiments.

They are sentiments which have become ideas, as is the case doubtless with all general ideas, and they are sentiments of great strength. The sovereignty of the people is the truth for him who believes in it, because it ought to be true, because it is a thing as full of majesty for him as was Cæsar in all his pomp for the ancient Roman, or Louis XIV. in all his glory for the man of the seventeenth century.

Equality is truth for him who believes, because it ought to be true, because it is justice, and because it would be infamous if justice and truth were not one. For the democrat, the world has ever been rising gradually, since its creation, towards the sovereignty of the people and the doctrine of equality; the latter contains the former, the former is destined to found the latter and has this mission for its purpose in life; together they constitute civilisation, and if they are not attained, there is a relapse into barbarism.

They are dogmas of faith. A dogma is an overmastering sentiment which has found expression in a formula. From these two dogmas everything that can be deduced without breach of logic is truth which it is our right and duty to proclaim.

We must add that the schoolmaster is urged in this same direction by sentiments of a less general character, which nevertheless have an influence of their own. He is placed in his commune in direct opposition to the priest, the only person very often who is, like himself, in that place a man of some little education. Hence rivalry and a struggle for influence. Now the priest, by a series of historical incidents, is a more or less warm partisan sometimes of monarchy but almost always of aristocracy. He is a member of a body that once was an estate of the realm, and he is persuaded that his corporation is still an estate of the realm, notwithstanding all that has happened. If the existing order is regulated by the *concordat*, the existing order recognises his corporation as a body legitimatised by the State, since it treats it on the same terms as the magistracy and the army. If the existing order is one based on the separation of State and Church, his corporation appears to him still more to be an estate of the realm, because being forced into an attitude of solid organisation, and recognising no limitations of frontier, it becomes a collective personage which, not without peril, but also not without a certain measure of success, has often ventured to cross swords with the State itself.

As the priest then belongs to an order endowed with an historic authority which is nevertheless distinct from, and in no wise a delegation from, the authority of the people, the priest cannot fail more or less definitely and consciously to adopt an attitude of mind favourable to aristocracy.

The school teacher, his rival, is thrown then all the more inevitably towards the adoption of democratic principles, and he embraces them with a fervour into which enters jealousy quite as much as conviction. They mean more to him than even to an eighteenth century philosopher, because he has a much greater personal interest in believing them, the interest of personal dislike and animosity; for it is his belief that everything taught by the priest is the pure invention of ingenious oppressors who wish to enslave the people in order to consolidate their own tyranny; and that is his reason for professing philosophical ideas resuscitated from the teaching of Diderot, and Holbach. For the school teacher it is almost inconceivable that the priest should be anything but a rascal.

"Atheism is aristocratic," said Robespierre, thinking of Rousseau. Atheism is democratic, say our present-day school teachers. Whence comes this difference of opinion? First because it was fashionable among the great lords of the eighteenth century to be libertines and free-thinkers, but among the people the belief in God was unanimous. Secondly, because the priests of our day, for the reasons which I have given and from remembrance of the persecutions suffered by their Church at the date of the first triumphs of democracy, have remained aristocrats or have become so even more firmly than they ever were before. Atheism then has become democratic as a weapon against the deists who are generally aristocrats.

Besides, atheism fits in very well, whatever Robespierre may have thought, with the general sentiments of the baser demagogy. To be restrained by nothing, to be limited by nothing, that is the dominant idea of the people, or rather it is the dominant idea of the democrat for the people, that it should be restrained by nothing and limited by nothing in its sovereign power. Now God is a limit, God is a restraint. And just as the democrat will not admit of a secular constitution which the people could not destroy and which would prevent him from making bad laws; just as the democrat will not submit—if we may adopt the terminology of Aristotle—to being governed by *laws*, to be governed that is by an ancient body of law which would check the people and obstruct it in its daily fabrication of *decrees*; so just in the same spirit the democrat does not admit of a God Who has issued His commandments, Who has issued His body of laws, anterior and superior to all the laws and all the decrees of men, and Who sets His limit on the legislative eccentricities of the people, on its capricious omnipotence, in a word, on the sovereignty of the people.

After Sedan, Bismarck was asked: "Now that Napoleon has fallen, on whom do you make war?" He replied: "On Louis XIV." So the democrat questioned on his atheism could reply: "I am warring against Moses."

This is the origin of the atheism of democrats and schoolmasters. This is the origin of the formula: "Neither God nor Master," which for the anarchist requires no correction nor supplement, which for the democrat has only to be modified: "Neither God nor Master, save the People."

At the end of one of his great political speeches in 1849 or 1850, Victor Hugo said: "In the future there will only be two powers; the People and God." The modern democrat has persuaded himself that if there be a God, the sovereignty of the people is infringed, if he believe in Him.

Lastly, the school teacher is confirmed in his democratic sentiments, in all his democratic sentiments, by the political position which has been made for him in France. It is a strange thing, a disconcerting anomaly, that the Governments of the nineteenth century (especially, we must do it this justice, the present Government), have very handsomely respected the liberty of professors of higher education, and of secondary education, and have not in the very slightest degree respected the liberty of the teachers of elementary education. The professor of higher education, especially since 1870, can teach exactly what he pleases, except immorality and contempt of our country and its laws. He can even discuss our laws, provided always that he maintains the principle that, such as they are, they ought to be obeyed till they are repealed. His liberty as to his opinions political, social and religious is complete. It is only occasionally constrained by the disorderly demonstrations of his students. The professor of secondary education enjoys a liberty almost equally wide. He is subject, but only in an extremely liberal fashion, to a programme or syllabus of studies. As to the spirit in which he conducts his work he is practically never molested. He is given a free hand.

Nor has it ever occurred to any Government to ask a professor of higher and secondary education how he votes at political elections, still less to require him to canvass in favour of the candidates agreeable to the Government.

When, however, we pass to elementary education we see everything is changed. The elementary teacher is not appointed by his natural chief, the *recteur* or Minister of Public Education, he is appointed by the *préfet*, that is by the Minister of the Interior, the political head of the Government. In other words, this is the same process as the appointment of officials by the people, described a few pages back, but with one intermediary the less. It is pre-eminently the Minister of the Interior who represents the political will of the nation at any given date. And it is the Minister of the Interior who through his *préfets* appoints the elementary school teacher. It is then the political will of the nation which chooses the school teachers. It would be impossible to convey to them more clearly (which is only fair, for people should be made to understand their duties) that they are chosen for considerations of politics and that they ought to consider themselves as political agents.

And indeed they are nothing else, or perhaps we should say they are something else but above all they are politicians. The schoolteachers depend on the *préfets* and the *préfets* depend much on the deputies, yet it is not the deputies who appoint them, but it is they who can remove them, who can get them promoted or disgraced, who by constant removals can reduce them to destitution. Surely, every candid person will exclaim, given the difficult and scandalous situation in which they are put by the hand which appoints them, they ought at least to have the guarantee and assurance, very relative and ineffectual though it be, of irremovability. But they have not got it. The professors of higher education who do not require it have got it, the professors of secondary education have it to all intents and purposes. The elementary school teacher has it not.

He is, therefore, delivered over to the politicians who make of him an electioneering agent, who reckon him as such, and who would never pardon him if he failed them.

The result is that the majority of school teachers are demagogues because they like it, and with magnificent enthusiasm and passion. The minority who have no turn for demagogy are demagogues though they do not like it, and because they are forced by necessity.

Even those who have no disposition that way become demagogues in the end, for that is the way of the world. "In the heat of the *mêlée*," said Augier, "there are no mercenaries." Our school teachers, thrown, sometimes against their will, into the battle, forced at least to appear to be fighting, receive knocks and when they have received them, they become attached to the cause on whose behalf they have suffered. We always end by having the opinions which are attributed to us, and being taken for a demagogue the moment he arrives at his village, the young school teacher, not daring to say anything to the contrary, and being very ill received by all other parties, naturally becomes a demagogue with some show of conviction the very next year.

So the democracy receives no instruction that does not confirm and strengthen it in its errors.

For its good some one ought to teach it not to believe itself omnipotent, to have scruples as to its omnipotence, and to believe that this omnipotence should have defined limits; it is taught without reserve the dogma of the unlimited sovereignty of the people.

For its good it should believe that equality is so contrary to nature that we have no right to torture nature in order to establish real equality among men, and that the people which has established such a state of things, which is quite possible, must succumb to the fate of those who try to live exactly in opposition to the laws of nature. Instead, it is taught, and it is true enough, that equality is not possible, if it is not complete, if it is not thorough, that it ought to be applied to differences of fortune, social position, intelligence, perhaps even to our stature and personal appearance, and that no effort should be spared to bring all things to one absolute level.

For its good, since it is natural enough that it should dislike heavy taxation, sentiments of patriotism should be reinforced; it is taught on the contrary that military service is a painful legacy left by a hateful and barbarous past, and that it ought to disappear very soon before the warming rays of a peaceful civilisation.

In a word, to use again the language of Aristotle, the pure wine of democracy is poured out to the people as it was by the demagogues to the Athenians; and from the quarter whence a remedy might have been expected there come only incitements to deeper intoxication.

Aristotle has made yet another wise and profound observation on the question of equality: "*We must establish equality*," he said, "*in the passions rather than in the fortunes of men.*" And he adds: "And this equality can only be the fruit of education derived from the influence of good laws." That is indeed the point. Education should have but one object; to reduce the passions to equality, or rather to *equanimity*, and to a certain equilibrium of mind. The education given to modern democracy does not lead to this, but leads in the opposite direction.

CHAPTER XII.
THE DREAM.

What remedies can we apply to this modern disease, the worship of intellectual and moral incompetence? What is, as M. Fouillée puts it, the best way of avoiding the hidden rocks which threaten democracies? It is hard to say, for we have to do with an evil which can only be cured by itself, with an evil which is more than content with itself.

M. Fouillée (in the *Revue des Deux Mondes* of November, 1909) proposes an aristocratic Upper Chamber, that is to say, one that would represent all the competence of the country, inasmuch as it would be appointed by everything which is based on some particular form of excellence, the magistracy, the army, the university, the chambers of commerce, and so on.

Nothing could be better; but the consent of the democracy would be necessary, and it is precisely these incorporations of efficiency that the democracy cannot abide, looking on them, not without reason, as being in a sense aristocracies.

He proposes also an energetic intervention on the part of the State to restore public morality, action for the suppression of alcoholism, gambling and pornography.

Beyond the fact that his argument savours of reaction, for it recalls to us the programme of "moral order" of 1873, we must remark, as indeed M. Fouillée himself acknowledges, that the democratic State can hardly afford to kill the thing which enables it to live, to destroy its principal source of revenue. Democracy, as its most authoritative representatives have admitted, is not a cheap form of government. It has always been instituted with the hope, and partly with the expressed design, of being an economical government, and it has always been ruinous, because it requires a much larger number of partisans than other forms of government, and a smaller number of malcontents than other forms of government, and these partisans have to be remunerated in one fashion or another and the malcontents have to be silenced and bought in one way or another.

Democracy, whether ancient or modern, lives always in terror of tyrants who are always imminent or thought by it to be imminent. Against this possible tyrant who would govern with an energetic minority, the democracy requires an immense majority which it has to bind to it by the grant of many favours; it has also to detach from this tyrant the malcontents who would be his supporters if it did not disarm them by a still more lavish distribution of favours.

Democracy requires therefore plenty of money. It will find this by despoiling the wealthy as much as possible; but this is a very limited source of revenue, for the wealthy are not a numerous class. It will find it more easily, more abundantly also, by exploiting the vices of all, for all is a very numerous group. Hence the complaisance shown to drinking shops, which, as M. Fouillée remarks, it would be more dangerous for the Government to close than to close the churches. As the needs of the Government increase, as M. Fouillée predicts, without much doubt it will claim a monopoly in houses of ill-fame and in the publication of indecent literature; enterprises in which there would be money. And after all, tolerating such things for the profit of certain traders and annexing them to be worked for the profit of the State, is surely much the same thing from a moral point of view. And the financial operation would be much more beneficent in the second case than in the first.

M. Fouillée also argues that reform must come "from above and not from below," and that "the movement for regeneration can come from above and not from below."

I ask nothing better, but I ask also how is it going to be done? Inasmuch as everything depends upon the people, who, what, can influence the people except the people itself? Everything depends on the people, by what then can it be moved except by a force that is innate. We are here confronted—we are talking to a philosopher and can make use of scientific terms—with a Κινητὴς ἀκίνητος with a motive force which causes but does not receive motives.

A principle has disappeared, a prejudice if you like to call it so, the prejudice in favour of competence. We no longer think that the man who understands how to do a thing ought to be doing that thing, or ought to be chosen to do it. Hence, not only is everything mismanaged, but it seems impossible by any device to handle the matter effectually. We see no solution.

Nietzsche really has a horror of democracy; only like all energetic pessimists, who are not mere triflers, he used to say from time to time: "There are pessimists who are resigned and cowardly. We do not wish to be like them." When he would not take this view he persuaded himself to look at democracy through rose-coloured spectacles.

At times, looking at the matter from an æsthetic point of view, he used to say: "Intercourse with the people is as indispensable and refreshing as the contemplation of vigorous and healthy vegetation," and although this is in flagrant contradiction to all he has elsewhere said of the "bestial flock" and the "inhabitants of the swamp," the thought has a certain amount of sense in it. It signifies that instinct is a force, and that every force must be interesting to study; and further that, as such, it contains an active virtue, a principle of life, a nucleus of growth.

This, though vaguely expressed, is very possible. After all the crowd is only powerful by reason of numbers, and because it has been decided that numbers shall decide. It is an expedient; but an expedient cannot impart force to a thing that had it not before. Motive power, initiative, belongs to the man who has a plan, who makes his combination to achieve it, who perseveres and is patient and does not relinquish pursuit. If he is eliminated and reduced to impotence or to a minimum of usefulness, one does not see how the crowd, without him, can obtain its power of initiation. Further explanation is needed.

At another time, Nietzsche asks whether we ought not to respect the right, which after all belongs to the multitude, to direct itself according to an ideal—there are of course many ideals—and according to the ideal which is its own. Ought we to refuse to the masses the right to search out truth for themselves, the right to believe that they have found it when they come upon a faith that seems to them vital, a faith that is to them as their very life? The masses are the foundation on which all humanity rests, the basis of all culture. Deprived of them, what would become of the masters? It is to their interest that the masses should be happy. Let us be patient; let us grant to our insurgent slaves, our masters for the moment, the enjoyment of illusions which seem favourable to them.

So Nietzsche argues, but more often, for he returns on various occasions to this idea, led thereto by his customary aristocratic leanings, he speaks of democracy as of a form of decadence, as a necessary prelude to an aristocracy of the future. "A high civilisation can only be built upon a wide expanse of territory, upon a healthy and firmly consolidated mediocrity." [So he wrote in 1887. Ten years earlier he held that slavery had been the necessary condition of the high civilisation of Greece and Rome.] The only end, therefore, which at present, provisionally of course but still for a long time to come, we have to expect, must be the decadence of mankind—general decadence to a level mediocrity, for it is necessary to have a wide foundation on which a race of strong men can be reared. "The decadence of the European is the great process which we cannot hinder, which we ought rather to accelerate. It is the active cause at work which gives us hope of seeing the rise of a stronger race, a race which will possess in abundance those same qualities which are lacking to the degenerate vanishing species, strength of will, responsibility, self-reliance, the power of concentration...."

But how, out of this mediocrity of the crowd, a mediocrity which, as Nietzsche says, is always increasing, by what process natural or artificial can a new and superior race be created? Nietzsche seems to be recalling the theory, very disrespectful and very devoid of filial piety, by which Renan sought to explain his own genius. "A long line of obscure ancestors," he says, "has economised for me a store of intellectual energy," and he jots down in his note book certain suggestions, a little immature but still emitting a ray of light. "It is absurd," he says, "to imagine that this victory or survival of values (that is low values, values, that is, that seem to be mediocrity) can be antibiological: we must look for an explanation in the fact that they are probably of some vital importance to the maintenance of the type 'man' in the event of its being threatened by a preponderance of the feeble-minded and degenerate. Perhaps if things went otherwise, man would now be an extinct animal. The elevation of type is dangerous for the preservation of the species. Why? *Strong races are wasteful, we find ourselves here confronted with a problem of economy.*"

We perceive, in this train of reasoning, some inkling of what Nietzsche is trying to formulate as his solution of the difficulty. What is needed must be a natural process, a *vis medicatrix naturæ*. In the process of declining and falling, races practise a sort of thrift; they save and they economise. Then, if we may suppose that the quantity of energy of intellectual and moral power, *i.e.*, of "human values" at the disposal of the race is constant, the races that so act are creating in themselves a reserve which one day will irresistibly take shape in a chosen class. They are creating in their own bosom an *élite* which will one day emerge, they have conceived all unconsciously an aristocracy which will one day be born to be their ruler.

We always find in Nietzsche the theory of Schopenhauer, the theory of the great deceiver who leads the human race by the nose and who makes it do and, as if it liked it, that which it would never do if it knew where it was being led. It is very possible; still it remains that economy carried to an extreme, though it can lead to a reserve of force, may also lead, and perhaps much more surely, to a condition of anæmia; the annihilation of one set of competent people in order to prepare the way for races of competent people in the future, I do not know if this is a game inspired by the great deceiver, but it is a game which to me appears dangerous. We ought to be sure (and who is sure?) that the great deceiver does not abandon those who abandon themselves.

I have often said, without thinking of any metaphysical mythology, thinking indeed of the ambitious people whom we meet everywhere, and thinking only of giving them some good advice: "The best way to get there is to come down." Nothing could be more philosophical, Nietzsche would reply; it is even more true of peoples than of individuals: the best way for peoples to become one day great is to begin by growing smaller. I rather doubt it. There is no really solid reason to support the theory that feebleness cultivated with perseverance results in strength. Neither Greece nor Rome supply examples, nor did the democratic republic of Athens nor the democratic Cæsarism of Rome ever succeed in giving birth to an aristocracy of competence by a prolonged economy of values.

—They did not have the time.—

Ah yes, there is always that to be said.

It would perhaps be better to try to put the brake on democracy than to encourage this process of degeneration on the chance of a favourable resurrection. At least this is the course which presents itself most naturally to our mind, and which seems most consonant with duty.

When I say put the brake on democracy, it must be understood that I mean that it should put the brake on itself, for nothing else can stop it, when once it has made up its mind. It must be persuaded or left alone, and even persuasion is a rash experiment, for it dislikes being persuaded of anything but of its own omnipotence. It must be persuaded or left alone, for every other method would be still more useless.

It must be reminded that forms of government perish from the abandonment and also from the exaggeration of the principle from which their merit is derived, though this is a very superannuated maxim; that they perish by an abandonment of their principle because that principle is the historical reason of their coming into existence, and they perish by carrying their principle to excess, because there is no such thing as a principle that is absolutely good and sufficient in itself for regulating the complexity of the social machine.

What do we understand by the principle of a government? It is not that which makes it be such and such a thing, but that "which makes it act" in a particular way, as Montesquieu has remarked; that is, "the human passions which supply the motive forces of life." It is clear then that the passion for sovereignty, for equality, for incompetence, is not sufficient to give to a government a life which is at once complete and strong.

It is necessary to give to competence its part, or rather it is necessary to give competence one part, for I do not wish to argue that there is any question of right involved, I only affirm that it is a social necessity. It is necessary that competence, technical, intellectual, moral competence should be assigned its part to play, even though the sovereignty of the people should be limited and the principle of equality be somewhat abridged thereby.

A democratic element is essentially necessary to a people, an aristocratic element also is essentially necessary to a people.

A democratic element is essentially necessary to a people in order that the people should not feel itself to be a mere onlooker, but should realise that it is a part and an important part of the body social, and that the words "You are the nation, defend it," have a meaning. Otherwise the argument of the anti-patriot demagogues would be just. "What is the good of fighting for one set of masters against another set, since it will make no difference, only a change of masters?"

A democratic element is required in the government of a people, because it is very dangerous that the people should be an enigma. It is necessary to know what it thinks, what it feels, what it suffers, what it desires, what it fears, and what it hopes, and as this can only be learnt from the people itself, it is necessary that it should have a voice which can make itself heard.

This should be done in one way or another, either by a Chamber of its own which should be endowed with great authority, or by the presence in a single chamber of a considerable number of representatives of the people, or by plebiscites constitutionally instituted as necessary for the revision of the constitution and for laws of universal interest, or by the liberty of the press and the liberty of association and public meeting.

This would not perhaps be enough, but it would be almost enough. It is necessary that the people should be able to make known its wants, and to influence the decisions of the Government, in a word its voice should be heard and considered.

An aristocratic element is also necessary in a nation and in the government of a nation so that all that admits of precision shall not be smothered by that which is confused; so that what is exact shall not be obscured by what is vague, and so that its firm resolves shall not be shaken by vacillating and incoherent caprice.

Sometimes history itself makes an aristocracy—a fortunate circumstance for a nation! This forms a caste more or less exclusive, it has traditions, traditions more conservative of the laws than the laws themselves, and it embodies in itself all that there is of life, and energy and growth in the soul of a people. Sometimes history has failed to give us an aristocracy or that which history has made has disappeared. It is then that the people ought to draw one out of itself, it is then its duty to appropriate and preserve the high qualities to be found in men who have rendered service to the State or whose ancestors have rendered service to the State, who have special qualifications for each particular office and a moral efficiency for every form of public service.

These qualities constitute the acquired aptitude of an aristocracy for taking a part in the government; these qualities constitute its adaptation to its social environment, and to its special function in our social machinery and organisation. One might say that it is by these qualities that *it enters into and becomes part of the organism of which it is the material.* As John Stuart Mill has justly remarked, there cannot be an expert, well-managed democracy if democracy will not allow the expert to do the work which he alone can do.

What is wanted then and will always be wanted, even under socialism where, as I pointed out, there will still be an aristocracy though a more numerous one, is a blending of democracy and aristocracy; and here, though he wrote a long time ago, we shall find Aristotle is always right for he studied in a scientific spirit some hundred and fifty different constitutions.

He is an aristocrat, without concealment, as we have seen, but his final conclusions, whether he is speaking of Lacedæmon, which he did not like, or of Carthage, or in general terms, have always been in favour of mixed constitutions as ever the best. "There is," he says, "a manner of combining democracy and aristocracy—which consists in so arranging matters that both the distinguished citizens and the masses have what they want. The right of every man to aspire to magisterial appointments is a democratic principle, but the admission of distinguished citizens only is an aristocratic principle."

This blending of democracy and aristocracy makes a good constitution, but the union must not be one of mere juxtaposition which would serve only to put hostile elements within striking distance. I said a "blending" but the blending must be a real fusion. Our need is that in the management of public business aristocracy and democracy should be combined.

How? Well for many years I have been saying it and I hope I may live for many years longer to say it again. A healthy nation is one in which the aristocracy is "*demophil*," that is a lover of the people, and where the people is aristocratic in its leanings. Every people where the aristocracy is aristocratic and where the democracy is democratic is a people destined to perish promptly, because it does not understand what a people is, it has not got beyond the stage of knowing what is a class and perhaps not even as far as that.

Montesquieu praises highly the Athenians and the Romans for the following reason. "At Rome, although the people had the right of elevating plebeians to office, it could never bring itself to elect them; and although at Athens, it could by the law of Aristides, choose magistrates from all classes, it never happened according to Xenophon, that the lower people demanded the election of rulers who could injure its safety and its glory. The two instances are identical; only, as far as Athens is concerned, it signifies nothing, for at Athens everything was decided by plebiscite and in consequence the real rulers of Athens were the orators, in whom the people trusted, who enforced their decisions and really governed the city. At Rome the fact is of great importance for it was the elected magistrates who governed."

Republican Rome was indeed a country aristocratically governed which had, however, a democratic element in its constitution, and this democratic element, up to the time of the civil wars, was itself profoundly aristocratic, just as the aristocracy which was always open to an accession of members from the plebs was profoundly "demophil."

The institution of patron and client, even in the state of degeneracy which overtook it, is a phenomenon which I believe is well-nigh unique. It shows to what extent two classes felt the social necessity, the patriotic necessity of mutual support and of a recognition of an identity of interest.

A nation whose people is aristocratic and whose aristocracy is "demophil" is a healthy nation. Rome succeeded in the world because for five hundred years she enjoyed this social health.

An aristocratic people and a people-loving aristocracy. I had long believed the formula was of my own invention. I have just discovered, and I am in no way surprised, that Aristotle was before me. He quotes the oath which oligarchs take in certain cities. "I swear to be always the enemy of the people and never to counsel any thing that I do not know to be injurious to them." "This," he continues, "is the very opposite of what they ought to do or to pretend to do ... It is a political fault which is often committed in oligarchies as well as in democracies, and where the multitude has control of the laws, the demagogues make this mistake. In their combat against the rich, they always divide the State into two opposing parties. *In a democracy, on the contrary, the Government should profess to speak for the rich, and in oligarchies it should profess to speak in favour of the people."*

It is a Machiavelian counsel. Aristotle seems convinced that democrats can only *profess* to speak for the rich and that all we can expect from oligarchs is an appearance of speaking in favour of the people. Nevertheless he recognises clearly that for the peace and well-being of the commonwealth such should be their attitude.

There is something more profound than this. Aristocrats ought not only to appear but to be verily favourable to the demos, if they understand the interests of aristocracy itself, for aristocracy requires a base. Democrats also ought not only to appear but to be aristocratic if they understand the interests of democracy which requires a guide.

This reciprocity of good offices, this reciprocity of devotion, and this combination of effort are as necessary in modern as they were in ancient republics. It is, and we must coin a word to express it, a social "synergy" that is wanted. A union of all the vitalizing elements is as necessary in society as in the family. Every family that is divided must perish, every kingdom that is divided must perish.

I have said little of royalty which only indirectly concerns my subject. If we have seen instances of the institution of royalty firmly established, it is where the sentiment of royalty, appealing at once both to the aristocracy and to the people, has realised that "synergy" of the whole community of which we speak; it is where both, being united in devotion to one object, are led to be devoted to each other by reason of this convergence of their wills. *Eadem velle, eadem nolle amicitia est.*

There is no need of royalty for this. Royalty is our country itself personified in one man. In the identification of country and kingdom, we can and must arrive at this same union of the separate vitalities of the nation, at this same community and convergence of will. The humble must love their country in loving the great and the great must love their country in loving the humble; and so all classes must be at one in their hopes and in their fears. *Amicitia sit!*